Lattridus

5/30/88

Goggins Family Reunion

Central State University

Sunken gardens in the center of campus (in the 1950s)

CENTRAL STATE
UNIVERSITY

The First
One Hundred Years,
1887-1987

by **Lathardus Goggins**

Published by CENTRAL STATE UNIVERSITY

The paper in this book meets the guidelines for permanence and durability of the Committee on Production Guidelines for Book Longevity of the Council on Library Resources.

Library of Congress Cataloging in Publication Data

Goggins, Lathardus.
    Central State University: the first hundred years, 1887–1987.

    Bibliography: p.
    Includes index.
    1. Central State University (Wilberforce, Ohio)—History. I. Title.
LD881.C44G64   1987   378.771'74   87-3759
ISBN 0-87338-349-4 (alk. paper)

British Library Cataloguing in Publication data are available

This book is dedicated to the Central State University students of the past, the present, and the future—and especially to those who are, and who will be, friends and "alumni" of Central State University.

Contents

Foreword

For one hundred years, Central State University (CSU) has successfully molded the lives and destinies of thousands of industrious, talented men and women. From the very modest beginning of a single brick building erected in 1890, Central State University has become an established institution of higher learning which attracts scholars, administrators, faculty, and staff who possess exceptionally refined skills and specialized knowledge.

My personal romance with CSU began in the fall of 1952. As a seventeen-year-old high school senior, I visited the campus and it was love at first sight. Today, almost thirty-five years later, I feel an even greater sense of pride and gratitude; that pride is heightened in that my friend and colleague, Dr. Arthur Thomas, one of the most outstanding, talented, dedicated university administrators in the nation, serves as the sixth president of CSU. We can rejoice in the knowledge that CSU will continue to progress and excel as he carries forward a tradition of excellence established by the five presidents before him—Lionel Newsom, Lewis A. Jackson, Herman Branson, Harry E. Grove, and Charles Wesley.

Today, graduates of CSU are outstanding in their achievements in the fields of business, education, engineering, government, industry, law, medicine, religion, politics, the fine arts, and the military. It is time to record the bold adventure of Central State as a developing university of superior quality. Dr. Lathardus Goggins, whom I claim as a fellow Centralian, former schoolmate, valuable colleague, and good personal friend, has captured and illuminated the colorful dynamic history of this great university.

Dr. Goggins, Associate Professor of Geography at the University of Akron, holds Masters degrees in Geography, Technical Education–Micro Computers, and Urban Studies from the Ohio State University and the University of Akron; an Ed.S. in Pupil Personnel Administration from Kent State University; an Ed.D. in Higher Education Administration from the University of Akron; and a Ph.D. in History from St. John's University, New York. Additionally, he has traveled, studied, and conducted research in East Africa, India, and China. Dr. Goggins has spearheaded many grant awards programs and received numerous personal awards, including the National Association for Equal Opportunity in Higher Education 1984 Distinguished Alumni Award. These are just a few of the awards and accomplishments which establish Dr. Goggins as the ideal person to pen the first book which chronicles CSU's rich heritage.

I am very proud and honored to have been asked to contribute the Foreword for this history of Central State University. My exuberance in this effort is even more intensified for Dr. Goggins and I were classmates as we labored to earn our undergraduates degrees from CSU. With that beginning, we share a common love, interest, and commitment to the continued success of our Alma Mater.

As you read this book, may you reflect on the past but look to the future with anticipation, confidence, and excitement. As CSU moves to a second century of service, join us in becoming totally committed to contributing to a tradition of providing an atmosphere where academic excellence is a reality. With one hundred years upon which to build, Central State University looks forward to an even brighter future as a citadel of learning.

Dr. Douglas Covington
President, Alabama A. & M. University
Normal, Alabama
CSU Class of 1957

Preface

The purpose of this book will be sixfold: (a) to trace the development of Central State University as a pioneer institution for the higher education of blacks in Ohio, (b) to show the contribution of the institution to the cause of education, (c) to disclose the effect of the Central State University programs of study on the lives of the students, (d) to explain the influence of the institution on racial development in Ohio, (e) to show how the university has, since the split with Wilberforce University, attempted to meet the needs of a racial minority group in the state, and (f) to analyze the role of the six presidents in its development.

In carrying out the above objectives, an attempt was made to interpret the life and work of the institution for those who have been its students and for others who are interested in the higher education of blacks in America.

A comprehensive historical presentation of the founding, growth, and development of Central State University—one of the oldest black colleges in the United States continuously existing as a single institution—should be of interest to the faculty, alumni, and others associated with or connected to Central State, proponents of higher education for blacks, and the general public. The few pamphlets and other articles which have been published concerning the development of the institution lack much by way of an adequate treatment of significant events in the college's history and do not give a connected story of the institution's life.

No previous comprehensive, historical presentation of the facts concerning the development of Central State University has been written. References to the history of Central State University have been limited to a few paragraphs or pages in important historical works. Richard Demosthenes Kidd, in *Problems Encountered by the Faculty of Central State College, Wilberforce, Ohio,* an unpublished dissertation (1959), does not devote any space to the history of the institution.

If I have at any point, by inadvertence, misinterpreted or distorted the meaning of the interviews or data that were collected, I give a blanket apology; these are risks one runs when attempting to explain and interpret researched information.

A significant person in this endeavor has been Cathy Burwell. She has carried through, in a highly competent and painstakingly way, all the editing and technical details essential for the production of a publication of this type. I am both grateful for her contributions and admiring of her perspicacity in completing a series of demanding tasks.

I am under obligation to numerous persons for their assistance: M. Margaret Geib, Staff Cartographer at The University of Akron, who did all the sketches; and Cynthia Bronner, Hilda Kendron, Jennifer Turner and Alexis Williams, who did the typing and re-typing of the material.

Finally, I wish to acknowledge with special gratitude, the constant help and encouragement given by Walter G. Sellers, Director of University Relations and Alumni Affairs at Central State University.

one

The Origins and Early Growth of Wilberforce University, 1844·1896

Wilberforce University was begun on September 21, 1844 when the Ohio Conference of the African Methodist Episcopal Church selected a tract of land for what was then known as Union Seminary. It was intended for instruction of young men in the various branches of literature, science, agriculture, and mechanical arts, as well as for those who desired to prepare for the work of the ministry.

While Union Seminary was being built on a site twelve miles west of Columbus, another movement for the education of black persons in Ohio and neighboring free states was being fostered by the Methodist Episcopal church. In September 1853 the Cincinnati conference of that church appointed a committee on the "Elevation of Colored People." Study by this committee led to a church endorsement of an institution to be called Ohio African University. The present site at Wilberforce (then called Tawawa Springs) was chosen, a governing board and president were selected, and the school was opened in 1856.

By 1860, Ohio African University had an enrollment of over two hundred students at the high school and college levels combined. However, as the Civil War progressed, these numbers dwindled, and a corresponding drop in financial support forced the school to close in June 1862. The board of trustees, saddled with a $10,000 debt and little likelihood of relieving it, was about to sell the property to the state for use as an asylum when, at the last moment, in March of the following year, Bishop Daniel A. Payne of the African Methodist Episcopal church suggested that the Wilberforce location would be a preferable one for Union Seminary.

Although he had neither the permission of the church nor the money, Payne agreed to buy the school for the price of its debt. Money was raised, and the operation of Union Seminary was moved. The grounds, buildings, and equipment were purchased, and control of the school passed into the hands of black church officials.

Reopening in the spring of 1863 with Payne as president, the newly named Wilberforce University was soon brought into the fold of the AME church, which controlled its affairs and set the tone for its campus life. Four governing principles had been laid down for its development by Bishop Payne at the time the university reopened: (1) the institution was to be dedicated to a broad preparatory and collegiate liberal arts curriculum with a heavy emphasis on religious training; (2) students and faculty were expected to conduct themselves with iron discipline and religious piety;[1] (3) neither racial nor sexual discrimination was to be allowed in admissions or hiring; and (4) in order to keep the institution free of sectarianism, all evangelical churches were to be represented on the board of trustees.

The university did not reach most of these goals. Through rigid rules, the administration was able to control personal behavior, but in spite of Payne's desires, it quickly became an AME institution with a predominantly black faculty and an all-black student body. In addition, though the board of trustees was mixed by race and religion, the majority were black Methodists. In 1873, for example, 91 of 110 members of the immense board of trustees were members of the AME church; the remaining board members were white and black Baptists.

Signs of revival did appear during Wilberforce's first year as an AME institution. Under Payne's forceful leadership, the student body began to grow, and the debt was almost retired. Then, in mid-April 1865, while students and faculty were in nearby Xenia attending a celebration of the fall of the Confederacy, a disaster struck. Arsonists set fire to the school's main building, a large frame structure built as a resort hotel, which had served as a combination lecture and classroom facility, dormitory, and dining hall. Though the building was valued at $60,000, it was insured for only $8,000.

With a zeal and a genius for improvisation which the University was to show in all its financial crises, the task of rebuilding began immediately. An agent was employed to travel the country in search of financial contributions. Within a few years the agent had contributions from some of the wealthiest and most powerful men in America and the promise of $10,000 from the wills of Salmon P. Chase, governor of Ohio, and

2

Charles Avery, a Pittsburgh philanthropist. For a number of years, the Society for the Promotion of Collegiate and Theological Studies in the West and the American Unitarian Association made substantial annual donations.

Other white churches and charitable organizations gave generously. Collections were taken up in black churches and among black fraternal and benevolent organizations. All of these efforts were eclipsed though by a successful campaign in 1869-70 which enlisted the support of the Ohio General Assembly and members of the state congressional delegation. This campaign obtained from the Freedman's Bureau through the Congress of the United States $28,000 in funds available to schools for training teachers to work among the Southern freedmen.

Even though the AME church had commitments to some ten to fifteen other church-operated and church-affiliated schools, colleges, universities, and seminaries throughout the nation, it too agreed to help place Wilberforce on a sounder footing. For many years, it would be argued that Wilberforce's excellence relative to the other church schools entitled it to a significantly larger share of the AME funds for education. Unfortunately, however, the relatively poor church had little to give any of these institutions once it agreed to divide its money among all of them. In spite of the small sums involved, the church remained a leading source of funds for the university.

While the campus was undergoing reconstruction, thought was also given to restructuring the educational goals of Wilberforce. During the late 1860s and the early 1870s, the curriculum was systematized and broadened to include classics, science, theology, music, and law courses. At the same time, programs were retained and further developed for the training of school teachers. Enrollments rose in both the preparatory and collegiate divisions. Though the preparatory division continued to have a slight majority of the students until the World War I years, the latter division began in the early 1870s to send out graduates, at a slow but steady pace, to preach in the nation's AME churches and to teach in public schools.

Yet problems remained. The faculty was understaffed and overworked. Mary Church Terrell, looking back on the two years she spent as a teacher at Wilberforce during the 1880s, remembered:

> I taught everything from French to mineralogy in the college department to reading and writing in the preparatory department. . . . In addition to teaching five courses in subjects totally dissimilar, I was secretary to the faculty . . . and

3

played the organ for the church services every Sunday morning and evening and gave a night every week to choir rehearsal.[2]

Taxing working conditions, low wages, and the rigid code of moral and ethical behavior demanded by Bishop Payne and his successors no doubt helped to account for the considerable turnover of faculty. Several resignations—particularly damaging to the large teacher-training program—resulted from serious conflicts within the faculty, and between faculty members and Payne's successor, Rev. Benjamin Lee, a man who lacked Payne's charisma. This turnover caused some parents to lose faith in the stability of the university.

The most serious problem for the school's future was its continued dependence on random benevolence to supplement the pittance which the church could provide. Having neither an endowment fund of any significant size nor a large group of affluent alumni, Wilberforce administrators found it impossible to plan any long-range programs to govern the growth and development of the university. As if these funding difficulties were not serious enough, by the mid-1880s its debts were mounting, reaching over $9,000 in 1884, and teachers were owed $2,000 in back salaries. In 1885 the board of trustees authorized the mortgaging of the property and debated closing the university.

President Lee and, after 1884, his successor S.T. Mitchell dealt with regular financial crises. Mitchell, a teacher and principal from the black public schools of southwestern Ohio and the first lay president of Wilberforce, found soon after assuming office that the major sources of funds of the late 1860s had virtually vanished. Old friends had died, and charitable organizations of the Reconstruction years had either ceased to exist or were dedicating energy and resources exclusively to the southern freedmen. Clearly, a new strategy was needed for raising funds.

It was at this time that President Mitchell, an inner circle of administrators, and several of the younger faculty members mounted a campaign for the creation of a state-financed department at Wilberforce. In this effort, they tapped both the residual white benevolence left over from the Reconstruction era and the healthy respect of white politicians for the state's black vote, which during the 1880s was seen by both parties as the balance of power in state elections as well as in some municipal, county, and congressional contests. While most blacks were traditionally Republican, when the issue was important enough some black leaders were not above an occasional flirtation with the Ohio Democratic party (in spite of its links with Southern Democrats). And, whatever their feelings about blacks, Ohio's white Democratic politicians were colorblind when it came to seeking votes. Thus Republicans could not afford to be lax in rewarding black voters for their usual loyalty to the party. Such political independence produced a substantial part of the gains Ohio Negroes made during the late nineteenth century in the improvement of their civic status.[3]

In their pursuit of state funds, Wilberforce officials showed themselves to be adept at manipulating white benevolence and self-interest. The first step in their campaign was successful. In 1885, they secured the nomination and election of Rev. Benjamin Arnett to the state legislature. Rev. Arnett, a power in Republican politics both because of his church connections and his forceful personality, guided Wilberforce's plea through the legislature in 1886-87. In addition, a memorial with the signatures of all of the state's major politicians of both parties and the most prominent Ohioans in the professions and businesses was presented to the legislature in behalf of Wilberforce.

Little if any precedent existed in either the North or the South for the arrangement which Wilberforce secured from the Ohio legislature on March 19, 1887, linking a private sectarian institution and the state.[4] In exchange for Wilberforce's promise to provide buildings and teacher-training resources, the state agreed to finance a "Combined Normal and Industrial Department at Wilberforce University." The use of the word "at," rather than "of" or "for" was intentional, because the legislature left little doubt, however great its desire to aid the recovery of the struggling black university, that the new department was to be legally separate from the university and in the control of the public. The department was to be directed by a separate board of trustees, five to be named by the governor of Ohio, and four by the AME church, which was charged with protecting the state investment by maintaining "exclusive authority, direction, and control over the operation and conduct" of the department. This unit offered courses in vocational and teacher training, while the church unit offered courses in the liberal arts and was governed by a church-appointed board. At this time, the state pledged $5,000 per annum for 1887 and 1888 to the support of this department.

No provision was made for regular funding out of the general tax levy for education. Thereafter, the department trustees were to make annual estimates of expenses which were to be presented to, and reviewed by, the general assembly. To ensure that the department would benefit all Ohioans, state legislators from each of Ohio's eighty-eight counties were permitted to send one student from their district tuition free. Though no

5

racial stipulations were made at the time, it was generally believed that only blacks would wish to attend an institution connected with a black university and located in an overwhelmingly black community.

From the beginning, the agreement was fraught with the potential for misunderstanding and conflict between the state, the university, and the church over questions of the day-to-day control of the department's students, faculty, and resources. As the years passed and conflicts arose more frequently, the state moved to tighten its control. But it would still be some time before such conflicts became serious. In the first five years, with small budgets, few students, and the understandable chaos of early organization, the ambiguities of the arrangement remained largely hidden. The university took effective charge of establishing the department, easily and efficiently transferring the head of the university's normal department, Sarah Beirce Scarborough, to the principalship. Mrs. Scarborough was the wife of the distinguished classicist, President William Sanders Scarborough, and herself a translator of Lamartine. The president of the university acted as the department's superintendent. In this setting, given the already existing ambiguities inherent in the arrangement, it was not surprising that many inside and outside of the Wilberforce community would slowly come to see an organic unity between the church-affiliated school and the state-financed department on its campus. In the meantime, however, the university's financial crises were eased by the infusion of state funds into the institution's largest department, its normal school.[5]

Surprisingly, little attention appears to have been given by the black press to the struggle of the university for state aid or to the implications of the bargain struck between Wilberforce and the state. Perhaps this was understandable, for the 1880s were years of intense struggle and achievement in the black community's quest for political recognition and civil rights. Wilberforce's success in winning state aid and white liberal support, coupled with a respect for the black vote, was an important factor in the increasing number of blacks who sat in the state legislature and held state and local patronage positions during the decade, as well as in the passage in 1884 of a state civil rights law and the repeal in 1887 of anti-miscegenation legislation. Ironically, the same legislature which had passed the appropriation to help a dying black university retain its identity provided the outstanding integration victory of the decade—the repeal in 1887 of the state's separate public school law. Furthermore, as Ohio blacks concentrated on the public school issue, relatively little thought was given to higher education. For them, it was enough that almost all of the state's major private and public colleges and universities were open to those blacks who wished and could afford to attend. Few blacks were in attendance at these institutions, however, and most Ohio blacks appear to have seen quality, integrated education at the elementary and high school levels as the most important racial goal of the period.

While blacks were not universally enthusiastic about school integration—a minority arguing that many black teachers would lose their jobs and that black students needed black teachers—all were impressed by the achievements of the decade in wiping the state's laws free of the stain of color prejudice. School integration offered the additional possibility that in mixing with one another at an early age the children of both races would learn to live together. Reinforcing the correctness of this course was the fact that, in other northern states during the decade of the 1880s, blacks had used their vote and the goodwill of tolerant whites to similar ends. These were years of optimism for many northern black leaders, a period before the serious decline of race relations in the South and the increased rigidity of the color line in the North during the 1890s and after the turn of the century. Then it was still considered realistic to trust in the possibility of a gradual assimilation into the mainstream of American society. Harry C. Smith, the young editor of the black *Cleveland Gazette,* wrote of a "revolution" that had been taking place in race relations in the last decades, which he believed could only be furthered by integrated education. "Revolutions never go backward," Smith wrote hopefully, adding, "Education has ever been the handmaiden of freedom, progress, and reform."[6]

Many northern black leaders who came of age in the 1870s and 1880s developed a new racial strategy to fit these perceived conditions. This strategy was a slow but steady widening of the boundaries of racial equality and integration. The central tendency in their thought during these years was that an intelligent application of existing egalitarian legislation, a pragmatic use of the black vote in the North where its exercise was unfettered, the assimilation by blacks of the best standards of the American middle class, and alliances with racially tolerant and powerful whites would all help to consolidate and expand upon the gains made in the North and aid in the redemption of the South. To the extent that there was any unity among northern black leaders, it was formed around such a program. This strategy, of course, reflected the experiences and ideas of the white-influenced social classes out of which the northern black leaders of that day had developed. Their goals were dual: to find a formula for uplifting the masses and to work individually for acceptance by the white majority.

While few northern black leaders would have argued for the total abandonment of exclusively black social institutions—churches, fraternal orders, and benevolent societies—some questioned the continuance of voluntary separation. Harry C. Smith, for example, questioned the utility of all-Negro state and regional conventions—legacies, he implied, of the antebellum struggle against slavery and the northern black laws. Writing in 1885, Smith argued that blacks should seek entrance into the organizations and movements of the larger society. He explained "We still have our grievances, but instead of holding black men's conventions, let us meet each other, white and black in our representative gatherings and there fight it out on the line."[7]

It is a testimony to how comfortably and how far many Ohio black leaders sensed they had traveled on the road to full citizenship that they viewed Wilberforce's 1891 claim to federal money, on behalf of the combined normal and industrial department, as a direct threat to this integrative racial strategy. Neither the university's 1869-70 campaign for federal funds from the Freedman's Bureau nor its efforts in 1886-87 for state aid had elicited any such charge from blacks that the university was jeopardizing the future of the race.

The university's 1891 claim was based on federal legislation passed in 1890 to supplement funds made available by the Morrill Act of 1862 for the creation of public agricultural and mechanical colleges. Known as the second Morrill Act, the 1890 legislation appropriated $25,000 per annum for the further support of colleges established under the earlier law. The driving forces behind the second Morrill Act were the National Association of Land Grant Colleges and individual institutions (such as The Ohio State University) which had developed out of the 1862 law. Special provision was made, however, for the nation's black public colleges, which were not a product of the Morrill Act but were involved in mechanical and agricultural studies. Senator Thomas Pugh of Alabama had inserted a clause in the law for the benefit of Booker T. Washington's Tuskegee Institute, providing that money would be available on the basis of a just distribution of funds between black and white schools and to all public black colleges involved in relevant fields.

Prior to the adjournment of the general assembly in 1890, state Senator W. T. Wallace introduced a bill, to be taken up immediately upon reconvening in 1891, accepting the funds made available by the second Morrill

Act and granting them to The Ohio State University. Soon after, Wilberforce's President Mitchell, with consent of the faculties and trustees of both Wilberforce and the state-funded Combined Normal and Industrial Department, announced an intention to fight the Wallace bill. He proposed instead an equal division of funds between The Ohio State University and the Combined Normal and Industrial Department under the terms of the Pugh clause. Such an annual subsidy would have placed the state-funded department on a footing more secure and more conducive to growth than anything the state legislature had previously suggested for the department's future.

An additional factor in Wilberforce's claim was that the university was again threatened with the prospect of a relatively substantial loss of income due to the church's decision to separate the theology department from the college and establish it as an independent seminary on the campus. Ironically, the decision was in part an after-the-fact response to the creation of the Combined Normal and Industrial Department. After the establishment of the department, the bishops had become sensitive to the prospect of the church/state separation issue being raised—possibly to the detriment of both the church and the university. Perhaps too the church/ state separation issue only served as a rationale for resolving an older dispute: for years both bishops and ministers had been arguing that Wilberforce-educated ministers were too freely exposed to the liberal arts and had an insufficiently rigorous theological training.

Whatever the weight of each of these factors, the opening of Payne Theological Seminary in June 1891 signaled a division of the relatively meager, but still essential funds provided for the university by the AME church. Thereafter, church funds were to be apportioned between the preparatory and collegiate divisions and the seminary without a compensating increase in the full appropriation. The implication for Wilberforce was a weakening of the liberal arts curriculum, which the expansion of the state-controlled facilities might have helped check by inclusion of certain liberal arts courses in the funding for the teacher-training program.

When, early in the 1891 legislative session, Wallace amended his bill in response to pressure from Wilberforce and its friends to provide that half of the federal funds be given to the state-funded department, battle lines were quickly drawn between a segment of the Ohio black community and the university and its supporters. In a long interview printed in both the *Cleveland Gazette* and the *New York Age,* state Representative John P. Green, a Cleveland attorney and prominent black Republican,

9

attempted to refute the legal bases of Wilberforce's claim and pointed to its dangerous implications for the race. Green's argument displayed some of the usual confusion between the university and the state-controlled facility on its campus; thus, Green raised the issue of separation of church and state. It is important to remember, however, that black critics of the claim, as well as most whites involved in the debate, rarely mentioned the Combined Normal and Industrial Department. While adding imprecision and an element of unreality to the discussion, this misconception of the department's status highlighted divisions and loyalties within the black community.

But these technical matters were little known, and Green's argument was carefully considered, providing in great part the basis for black opposition to the claim. For Green, the elevation of Ohio blacks to fuller citizenship, symbolized by their election to the state legislature during the 1880s and the repeal of the black laws, made Wilberforce an anachronism. Exclusively black, except for a few faculty members, and affiliated with a black church, the university no longer represented, in Green's opinion, the range of opportunities for participation in the larger society available to northern blacks. But by its claim to federal funds, Green argued, the university had gone from being simply anachronistic to being detrimental to the race. In presenting itself and the Combined Normal and Industrial Department as institutions analogous to the legally established, segregated public colleges of the South, the university was playing into the waiting hands of those northern bigots who wished to turn the clock back to the days of the antebellum black laws. Employing a domino theory of segregation, in which every tendency of blacks to separate themselves voluntarily from the larger society was a possible precedent for white-imposed segregation, Green contended that Wilberforce's claim would jeopardize the opportunity of blacks to attend other public and private colleges in Ohio and perhaps even threaten recently won public school integration. He also implied that both the university and the state-controlled department would be completely acceptable to him only as integrated institutions. Green closed his interview by calling upon young blacks to enter all colleges and universities in Ohio and asking their parents to petition the legislature against the Wilberforce claim in order to preserve their right to do so.[8]

Not all blacks were as outspoken as Green in their condemnation of Wilberforce's claim nor as willing to see the university lose its racial character. Some publicly expressed sorrow at having to take a stand against the university they saw as a symbol of black courage and hopes.

But most were as adamant as Green in the belief that recognition of either the university or the state-funded department as "northern Tuskegees" could only harm black aspirations for quality, integrated public education.

Smith's *Cleveland Gazette* dwelled on this theme but went beyond Green to imply that those who favored bringing back the color line in Ohio public schools were secretly responsible for pushing Wilberforce's claim. Smith pointed out that some of the petitions which had appeared in the state legislature calling for a division of the funds were from southern Ohio counties where whites continued to resist school integration in spite of the law. The fact that at least two of the petitions contained almost no black signatures increased Smith's fear that, in his words, there was "an Irishman in the wood pile."[9]

Similar fears were expressed by the resolutions of a black mass meeting in Cincinnati, which produced a petition of 900 signatures against a division of the funds. The same themes were also presented by speakers at a Columbus mass meeting attended by 500 blacks. Though the latter was ostensibly held to establish a community position on the issue, the tide was strongly against Wilberforce from the beginning; in fact, the call to meeting was entitled, "Shall Ohio Be Southernized?" The Columbus rally was addressed by the most prominent black Democrat in the state, Herbert Clark, and one of the most prominent northern black Republicans of the era, the aging Baptist minister, Rev. James Poindexter. Both men made strong speeches against a division of the funds.

The Columbus meeting was also addressed by representatives of Wilberforce who attempted in vain to present the university's case. They watched helplessly as the rally passed resolutions opposing the university. Yet Columbus blacks admitted that divisions existed within their ranks. One person interviewed claimed that for him "church membership influenced to a greater degree than race advancement." In truth, the AME church was using its considerable influence in behalf of the university. Ministers were urging their congregations to petition for the passage of the amended Wallace bill. In addition, church officials were in contact with members of the general assembly. Such efforts were by no means insignificant; the greater potential for opinion-molding power which white politicians attributed to the AME church as an Episcopal church (in comparison with the decentralized Negro Baptist organization) frequently led them to open their ears to the views of AME spokesmen.[10]

As if this intervention in secular affairs were not enough, church members were also charged by the AME with using unseemly tactics. The black affairs reporter for the *Columbus Ohio State Journal* claimed, for

11

example, that letters had been sent to the *Cleveland Gazette* by AME members in which they threatened to organize a "boycott" of the paper unless Harry Smith changed his stand against the university. Smith neither affirmed nor denied these allegations, but just their presence embittered the debate considerably. Such charges no doubt also increased the commitment of non-Methodist blacks to oppose the university—not only out of sectarian rivalry, but also out of a genuine wariness of the expanded secular influence which continued public recognition of the university might give this already aggressive church.

The question of a division of the funds split the legislature deeply during the early weeks of debate. The upper house seemed nearly unanimous in its approval of the amended Wallace bill on March 18, and went so far as to approve, by a twenty-five to four margin, the creation of an agricultural department for the Combined Normal and Industrial Department in order that it might more strictly reflect the type of institution desired by the second Morrill Act. Senate Democrats and Republicans, in almost equal numbers and representing constituencies all over the state, voted in favor of the Wilberforce claim. As the lack of party and sectional alignments would suggest, rather than an organized movement to turn back the tide of integrated education in Ohio, the vote reflected a mixture of motives and perceptions. Impressed by the good work of Wilberforce, some senators no doubt saw aid for the struggling institution as a type of charity. Further buttressing this group was the feeling among some of its members that The Ohio State University had been blocking the development of all other state educational institutions by continually receiving the lion's share of public monies. Other senators were probably more concerned with the black vote and had been impressed by the superior lobbying power, relative to their opponents in the black community, of the AME church and the university.

In assessing the motives of the legislators, however, it would be difficult to find a racist component in their voting: both votes for and against the Wilberforce claim might be construed as resulting from racial prejudice. Given the trend of state action on racial questions during the previous decade, it is more than likely that race was secondary to educational and political considerations.

A majority of the House Committee on Agriculture, however, was set against House approval of the Wallace bill. Representing the interests of the state's farmers and The Ohio State University, the committee members demanded that extensive hearings be held to poll professional and interest-group opinion on the merits of dividing the funds. The decision to hold hearings gave The Ohio State University the opportunity which it had long desired to mount a counterattack. The Ohio State University officials had been angered and irritated from the beginning by the Wilberforce claim. They were surprised that it had gotten as much attention as it had. The Ohio State University, after all, had never drawn the color line against black students, though there were only some eleven of them in attendance in 1891. It certainly had the most respected and promising agricultural program among Ohio's colleges and universities. Armed with a letter from the United States secretary of the interior, written in late February, stating that a division of the funds might only occur when blacks were barred by law and custom from public institutions, state university officials mounted a most impressive lobby against the Wilberforce claim.

For blacks, believing that racial progress depended significantly on alliances with, or at the very least not alienating, powerful white opinion-makers, whether individual or corporate, the presence of major farm and labor spokesmen on behalf of The Ohio State University must have increased a sense of anxiety over the racial costs of the Wilberforce claim. During the week-long hearings, testimony against division was given by national, state, and county Grange and Farmers' Alliance officials, the heads of both the State Board of Agriculture and the Labor Board, and the president of the United Mine Workers Union. In addition, former President Rutherford B. Hayes, an Ohio State University trustee and a known friend of black education, testified against division of the funds.

While these speakers denounced Wilberforce's claim to the funds as a serious threat to the development of the state university and the interests of Ohio workers and farmers, they also showed considerable sensitivity to the racial implications of the claim. S. H. Ellis, the president of the Ohio Grange, echoed the sentiments of several other farm leaders when he protested vigorously any attempt to draw the color line in any of Ohio's schools. To the applause of black spectators at the hearings, he denounced what he said were the efforts of some black men to aid in spreading segregation across the North.

In response to these criticisms, S. T. Mitchell of Wilberforce and several black and white trustees of the Combined Normal and Industrial Department appeared in order to clarify the relationship among the church, the university, and the state—a continuing source of confusion and anti-Wilberforce sentiment. Mitchell was not insensitive to the fears of segregation expressed in some testimonies. He pleaded, however, for realism in assessing the needs of black students who did not attend The

13

Ohio State University in significant numbers but did attend Wilberforce and the Combined Normal and Industrial Department. The implication, no doubt, was that they would continue to express this preference no matter what other opportunities were available to them.

With the hearings, the tide had begun to turn against Wilberforce. Important defections were occurring among such prominent Wilberforce supporters as Senator Sherman, and anti-Wilberforce blacks were stepping up the pace of petitioning and lobbying against a division of the funds. When the bill reached the floor of the House in late April, it was expected that it would be amended to exclude a recognition of the Combined Normal and Industrial Department. While the amendment elicited some spirited debate in favor of Wilberforce, the vote in its favor was decisive. Fourteen of the fifty-four Republicans in the chamber and thirty-seven of sixty Democrats voted to refer the bill to a committee of one for amendment. Many other Republicans, torn between moral conviction and political calculation, showed a considerable fear of alienating black constituents: seventeen voted against referral, while twenty-three (43 percent of the Republicans in the House) absented themselves for the crucial vote. The House then voted sixty-one to sixteen, with no significant change in party or sectional alignments, to accept the entire bill.

While Wilberforce partisans in the Senate continued their fight for division of the funds, a search was already under way among influential members of both houses for a compromise before the amended bill left the House on April 22. The senators were impressed with both the obvious disunity among blacks on the issue and the sizeable show of support for The Ohio State University by farm and labor groups. In addition, the time for adjournment was nearing, and there was considerable fear among the legislators that failure to act in 1891 would cause the funds to revert permanently to the federal government.

The form of a compromise had been apparent for several weeks. During the first week of April, former President Hayes had written S. T. Mitchell that although he was against the Wilberforce claim he would pledge to work for increased state aid for the Combined Normal and Industrial Department. He promised that in the long run this would yield more money than would the federal grant. An unconvincing eleventh-hour conversion to Wilberforce's cause by Representative John P. Green, which earned him bitter criticism from The Ohio press, also signaled an effort to obtain increased state funds. Green's change in position appeared to come suddenly when he delivered a long, unexpected speech in the

House describing the university's needs and the work of the state-funded department. Actually, however, Green had consulted with Cleveland's black political leaders, including Harry Smith, before his speech and had obtained their approval for a compromise similar to the one Hayes had described.

It remained for two Republican senators to work out an agreement by which all the federal funds would be assigned to The Ohio State University and the state department at Wilberforce would receive larger state appropriations. The bill assigning the funds to The Ohio State University received near unanimous vote in both houses. Funds for the Combined Normal and Industrial Department, however, had to await the 1892 legislative session, at which time the state appropriation for the department was raised from the $2,000 received in 1889 (the year of the last state grant) to $16,000. Still larger sums were appropriated in 1894 and 1896. In the latter year, an arrangement was made by which the department would be supported permanently through a direct tax levy rather than through occasional legislative appropriations.

Although both sides acquiesced in the compromise, the future relationship between the university, the state, and the Combined Normal and Industrial Department failed to live up to the expectations of Wilberforce officials and realized some of the worst fears of their black opponents. As the result of increased state funding, the state-controlled department grew yearly until it represented an investment of hundreds of thousands of dollars on the part of the state. Its modern physical plant and the size of its campus, faculty, and student body eventually surpassed those of Wilberforce University. This growing state investment brought with it increasing demands that the legislature assert ultimate control over the affairs of the department and check the influence of the university and the church.

Thus, as the result of accumulated legislative acts and decisions by the board of trustees,[11] the power over the destiny of the department came to reside more with its trustees and less with Wilberforce officials. The first sign of the movement toward increased state control came, not surprisingly, in 1896, the year when the funding of the department through direct taxation was approved. In that year, the legislature changed the composition of the departmental board of trustees so that a majority were gubernatorial appointees. Also in 1896, by action of the department's board of trustees, the office of the superintendent of the department was separated from the office of the president of Wilberforce. As the depart-

15

ment increasingly became an entity of its own, the financial benefits derived by the university from its presence on the campus decreased significantly. Wilberforce University was, therefore, left as it had been before the creation of the state-funded department: to raise its own funds amid the uncertain avenues of church and private donations.

two

The Dissolution of a Historic Relationship, 1930·1951

Still, Wilberforce held its own over the years. Many resources were shared, with or without official intervention, but a more significant overlap in funding began in 1930. The church-supported unit had been experiencing ever greater financial difficulties resulting not only in the growing indebtedness of the university, but in teachers not receiving salaries. To alleviate this problem, in 1930, under the administration of Gilbert Jones, arrangements were made for the State of Ohio to pay the church unit a certain amount of money annually as tuition for those students enrolled in general education courses conducted by the church-supported unit. This made it possible for teachers again to receive their regular salaries.

Just two years later, Charles Wesley, then forty-one, was nominated for the Wilberforce presidency. After less than a month's on-site investigation of the school's situation, he declined the offer. He found a campus marked by "division, hostility, jealousy, envy and error."[1] During the years between Wesley's refusal and his eventual acceptance of the presidency, however, a significant technical change came about regarding the name of the school. The second period in the history of the college officially began on May 13, 1941, with the following action by the general assembly:

On and after the taking effect of this act the Combined Normal and Industrial Department established under the provisions of an act to aid in the establishment and maintenance of a Combined Normal and Industrial Department at Wilberforce University, Greene County, Ohio, passed March 19, 1887, shall be known as the College of Education and Industrial Arts at Wilberforce University, Greene County, Ohio.[2]

The result of this apparently minor change was to create a greater structural equality between the two parts of the school; no longer did the larger, wealthier state-supported unit appear to be merely a part of Wilberforce University.

Ten years later the offer to lead Wilberforce University as president was again made to Wesley by Bishop Reverdy C. Ransom (who continued to maintain a considerable amount of political clout at the university) and by the acting president, Bishop R. R. Wright, Jr. In a conversation with Bishop Wright, who was visiting Washington, D.C., Wesley showed some interest in the position. However, the next day he wrote Bishop Ransom, saying:

> I have thought prayerfully and carefully over your request for me to consider the presidency of Wilberforce University. I have reached the conclusion of requesting that my name be not included among those submitted to the University Trustees for vote at this time. I am interested in Education and particularly in Wilberforce University for what it stands in tradition, history and promise; but I am not interested in the partisan politics which I believe have developed within recent periods in this situation. The clash of personalities, the divisions in opinions and the alignments now operating in this institution, in spite of its future developments, outweigh the desire and urge which, I must acknowledge, profoundly challenge me. Frankly, I write this letter with some regret.[3]

Bishop Wright continued in his attempt to convince Wesley to accept. In a report to the Joint Executive Committee of Wilberforce, Bishop Wright asserted:

> Who shall be elected president of Wilberforce? . . . For the Wilberforce presidency is one of the most important and without doubt the most difficult college presidency among our people. On one thing all seem agreed (except a few politicians), that we should get the very best man possible for the place, and that everybody should give him the very fullest support. Without the latter assurance the position loses attraction for a really competent person.[4]

Bishop Wright further informed the committee that he had received applications for the position from fifteen persons.[5] Despite this, he concluded:

I am convinced that Dr. Wesley stands head and shoulders above all of them, and if he can be induced to change his mind and accept the responsibility here, we would have done the University a great service. Almost any terms he may require are worth acceding to, in my humble opinion.[6]

As a result of continued communication with Bishop R. R. Wright, Wesley decided to accept the offer if several conditions, outlined in a document entitled "Conditions of My Acceptance," could be met. These included a full confidence vote of the state and church trustees, salary and expense accounts, a residence for the president, executive power, and a several-year contract. The conditions ended with the following remarks:

It is agreed that I come to Wilberforce to engage in an educational program for the advancement of the institution and not to engage in politics nor "to run for the bishopric." If the above conditions are accepted, I shall be pleased to come to Wilberforce as President and to lead in an educational program for its advancement.[7]

Wesley was not fully comfortable with his decision. Accordingly, he asked Howard University President Mordecai Johnson for a leave of absence without compensation for the 1942–43 academic year.[8] In a letter to President Johnson, June 13, 1942, Wesley wrote:

I have just returned to the city this morning from Wilberforce, Ohio, where I was elected President of the University. I have given the offer considerable thought and have reached the conclusion to make a conditional acceptance. This acceptance is predicated upon the grant of a sabbatical leave for the academic year, 1942-43, from my position here as Professor of History and Dean of the Graduate School.

As you know, I have been at Howard University for twenty-eight years and I have some hesitation in abruptly breaking the ties which bind us to the University. However, there is a task which the leadership of the African Methodist Episcopal Church and the educational authorities of the State of Ohio feel that I can do for Wilberforce University. As a state-supported and church-controlled institution, it has numerous problems. The North Central Association, the accrediting agency for this area, has laid down certain stipulations which the institution will have to meet. One of these refers to the type of president. Fundamentally, I have no desire for this type of administration and have repeatedly rejected the offer. The emergency which has arisen at the present time makes it necessary for me to decide whether I will help to save this institution or again return a negative answer to the request of the leadership at the University.

I have decided to go if you and the Board of Trustees of Howard University will grant me a sabbatical leave, without salary, for this period of one year. During this time I hope to be able to accomplish some of the unification in administration and management which both University groups desire. My last sabbatical leave was in 1930–31 when I was awarded a Guggenheim Fellowship and was away on half salary. For the next year I desire to request this leave without salary. I hope that you will cooperate with me and make this recommendation to the Board of Trustees, for I am confident that you recognize the problem which I face with reference to annuity, retirement and the interruption of the scholarly pursuits which I have been following during the years. Such a leave will also indicate that there is no dissatisfaction either on my part or on the part of the University with the opportunities which I have had during my long period of service here at Howard University. This announcement to the public will also help to allay any criticism which may arise in the minds of those who would see a division where none exists. . . .[9]

This leave was granted, and in June 1942 Charles Wesley became the tenth president of Wilberforce University.

Wesley was fifty-one years old at the time and he had, already, a distinguished academic career behind him. In addition to his earned degrees—a B.A. in education from Fisk University in 1911, an M.A. from Yale University in 1913, and a Ph.D. from Harvard University in 1925—he had received several prestigious academic awards, including University Scholar at Yale and the Teachers Scholarship for 1920–21 at Harvard. He had also studied abroad—at the Guild Internationale in Paris in 1914, and in London from 1930 through 1931 as the recipient of a Guggenheim Fellowship. Eight honorary degrees (one of them a Doctor of Divinity degree from Wilberforce University in 1928) had been bestowed on him as well.

Nor was his background in teaching and administration an ordinary one. At Howard University, where he spent twenty-eight years, he made advancements on an average of once every two years. Beginning as an instructor of history, he moved through the professorial ranks within the history department. He then became, successively, dean of the College of Liberal Arts, director of Summer Sessions, and dean of the Graduate School.

His work as an author had also brought him renown. Of the more than thirty full-length books he authored or co-authored, five major works— *Negro Labor in the United States, 1850–1925; Richard Allen, Apostle of Freedom; Collapse of the Confederacy; The History of Alpha Phi Alpha;* and *A Manual of Research and Thesis Writing for Graduate Students—* had already been published in 1942.

DR. CHARLES H. WESLEY
PRESIDENT (1942)

Those who sought to bring him to Wilberforce undoubtedly viewed him as the perfect leader for the school—a man who had investigated, publicized, and evinced pride in his black heritage, but whose scholarly credentials were recognized in both the black and the white communities. Their hopes for Wesley were not unfounded.

With Wesley's assumption of the presidency, the university's fortunes began to improve. After less than a year, Wesley was characterized by Bishops John Gregg and Reverdy Ransom as "the best president Wilberforce ever had in its history." It was reported in *The Christian Recorder* that "Wilberforce is moving forward as never before with a unified program."[10]

In 1943, at the annual meeting of the Board of Advisers of the North Central Association in Chicago, the situation at Wilberforce was characterized as showing "marked improvements and the conditions for accreditation were completely removed by action of the Association."[11]

Wesley quickly gained a reputation for attempting to create a progressive and first-rate institution. Upon his suggestion, in June 1943, the university began an active "functioning student self-governing council" to handle student related matters in the university. The council was elected from each class by the students of that class, and four faculty members were appointed to it by the president.

Other structural changes included the creation of a summer school and the replacement of the semester system with the quarter system. This was done in order to attract teachers to the summer program and to initiate graduate programs for the benefit of teachers in service. Master's degree programs were offered. A reorganization plan also attempted to eliminate some of the duplication that existed between the church and state units. Departments were replaced with divisions, three in the College of Liberal Arts and four in the College of Education. Curriculum changes were made, including the introduction of courses in African culture and civilization.[12] The creation of an African museum was authorized.[13] Finally, a member of the state board of trustees, Ray Hughes, became the first such trustee also elected to the church board of trustees.

Wesley's programs and future plans for the university needed financing. His appeals before the state legislature in 1943 brought the school a million dollars to expand and to operate its facilities. Buildings were completely renovated, including the cafeteria and water supply unit. Almost half of the faculty and staff were tenured, and salaries in the church and state units were equalized.

In addition to state aid, Wesley appealed to the members of the church for financial support in order to "give a new emancipation to Wilberforce, now in chains." He further asserted in the nationwide appeal:

> There has been a rapid transition from education controlled by church to education controlled by state. Wars have been fought over this, and the issue is, Shall we allow the state to mold society, to fashion life and civilization . . . ?
>
> Wilberforce is facing a dilemma that has faced it for a decade, Do we surrender or do we carry on? We as a nation are soon going to be forced to decide if we want government influence to become the dominant factor in our Universities. The collegiate education at Wilberforce has made tremendous contributions to the advancement of Negro Life. . . .[14]

Wesley was interested in building Negro leadership, and at the Churches of America Conference, he told the delegates that American Mission boards were not only shortchanging on the work in Africa and Liberia, but that the money being spent out to be used to develop colored leaders for colored people and not to continue to have whites do the leading.[15]

With clarity and seriousness, Charles Wesley had addressed himself to a challenge that faced the black community. His analysis indicated a strategy of self-reliance and black control of black institutions.

In 1944, the college was admitted to the Inter-University Council of Ohio and thus became one of the six constituent institutions composing Ohio's public higher education body at that time. The college was accredited by and held membership in the following educational organizations: North Central Association of Colleges and Secondary Schools; Association of American Colleges; American Association of Colleges for Teacher Education; National Association of Schools of Social Administration; American Medical Association; Ohio College Association; Inter-University Council of Ohio; Ohio State Department of Education; Association of Colleges and Secondary Schools for Negroes; University of the State of New York; State Department of Education, New York; and Association of Teacher Education Institutions. As a result, its graduates have been accepted and their credits have been honored by institutions of national and international renown. Wesley's relationship with both church and state boards was apparently one of unity for two years.

However, events began to occur which caused concern. In August 1944, *The Afro-American* reported a situation in which the ousted president of Wilberforce, Dr. Ormonde Walker, was to be rehired. The bishops were seen as instrumental in that decision. Wesley was said to be unaware of the appointment and filed a protest against the action. Walker claimed that he had not intended to return to Wilberforce, but had been so induced by the bishops. Furthermore, Walker declared he had no intention of embarrassing Wesley. (And, in fact, he did not accept the position.) Support for Wesley in this situation came from a high church official, according to *The Afro-American,* which reported:

> Dr. Wesley is in many respects the ablest president the University has had, and one of the most progressive. But there is a move of politically minded bishops to replace him. There is no cause—no reason is needed.
>
> Some bishops lack stability. Do you know of any first class institution where trustees would remove two presidents and then put them back on the campus in subordinate jobs? What we are witnessing is rivalry among bishops to control jobs at Wilberforce.[16]

Throughout this dispute, Wesley maintained that he was successful in bringing harmony to the two boards and in gaining support of the state board for the coordination of administration, management, course offerings, and disbursements of funds. This was indeed a great achievement at Wilberforce. In fact, Wesley boasted on many occasions that his word was law insofar as that state board was concerned.

The dispute over church and state control continued to grow. It was quickly picked up by the local press. At issue in 1945 was Senate Bill 293, which would give the State of Ohio sole control over the hiring and firing of the Wilberforce president as well as the right to establish a state university for Negroes in Ohio. Supporting Wesley and the state board, the *Cleveland Call and Post* reported: "Too long has this office (the Presidency of Wilberforce) been used as a stepping stone to high elective church offices. Because of this condition, the school has suffered and if it were not for the aid given by the State of Ohio, there really wouldn't be any Wilberforce left."[17]

In opposition, the *Chicago Defender* charged: "Wesley and Attorney Ray Hughes are pursuing a course of action designed to gain control and domination over the church-controlled College of Liberal Arts. . . . This bill [SB 293] if passed would set up at Wilberforce a complete Jim Crow college on the soil of Ohio."[18] This bill was opposed by the bishops and the AME church because it would give the state the right to hire and fire the president of Wilberforce University.

The *Chicago Defender* reported that Wesley was the first president of Wilberforce to join forces with politicians in an effort to gain control of

Wilberforce for the state. In doing this, the *Defender* continued, "Wesley would be establishing a comfortable berth for himself and political patronage for politicians."[19]

Editors of the *Ohio State News* concurred, citing supporters of the bill as those who "would alleviate Ohio's white institutions of its black population." They further predicted that as the bill went, so would Wesley, because the Republicans who were supporters of it feared the AME church, the influence of the bishops, and the Negro vote.[20]

Wesley answered these accusations in an announcement entitled, "President Wesley Issues Statement Concerning Wilberforce." In this he stated:

> In 1942 I was informed that the executive situation has been changed. In response to the conditions of acceptance which I presented I was given the definite assurance by both boards that I would have their wholehearted support and cooperation in my administration as President of the entire University, and was so elected.
>
> It is because of this background in part that the bishop has charged that I have collaborated in the introduction of Senate Bill 293 which places in *law* the situation which was placed in *fact* in 1942. I will have no part in either the presentation, the advocacy or the defeat of the bill, [*sic*] but as president and citizen, I have an opinion upon the ten years of contrasting experience noted above. Instead of the University being made a political football by this bill, it prevents a president from being made the political football in the future as he was in the past. This is further emphasized when it is recalled that there have been three Presidents of Wilberforce in this ten-year period, and five actual changes in the Presidency. Perhaps there are reasons for these changes but the conclusion is inevitable that, the tenure of a Wilberforce president is not only insecure but of brief duration.
>
> My personal security at Wilberforce will not be affected one way or other by this bill but it will mean that personal manipulations from persons, within the shadows, will be less influential, and that attacks and criticisms must be objective, rather than personal. The state board, its chairman and individual members, is composed of the same fine group of persons as the university board. The former is no more a set of politicians than the latter. Name-calling in public does not make it more so. . . . But politics has no place in an educational institution. I hope that the Bishop will help us to get rid of it.
>
> All of the speech, action and writings of my career belie such an accusation. I want to build the best possible university for the youth of all races who will come to us.[21]

The real issue at Wilberforce was not Wesley's fitness, but the politicians' need to control the university through passage of Senate Bill 293.

In the words of Charles S. Spivey, member of the Wilberforce community for thirty-five years, "It's power they wanted and the rewards that went with it . . . the real issue was not Wesley, not the Board, not setting up another institution; these were smoke screens."[22]

In an attempt to eliminate the struggle for control of Wilberforce between state and church, the two trustee boards met and reactivated the Joint Executive Committee, previously formed in 1941. This committee of six trustees, three from each board, had been empowered by the state and church boards of trustees to have the "authority to regulate all matters where the interests of the College of Liberal Arts and the College of Education overlap and should be unified."[23]

With the reactivation of the Joint Executive Committee, conditions at Wilberforce remained relatively the same because of the constant "jockeying for control between the church and state boards." Despite this, the enrollment reached 1,480 in 1946, which was termed "overcrowded" by President Wesley. From 1942–43 to 1946–47 the Wilberforce faculty increased from 98 full-time personnel, 13 of whom were Ph.D.'s, to 120 full-time teachers, 16 of whom were Ph.D.'s.

The administration of Wilberforce required an increasing amount of Wesley's time. His speaking engagements were reduced and his academic research impeded (although his first two years at Wilberforce saw him publish seven articles, five on education and two on history). He accepted the restriction on his research with reservation, as is shown in a letter to Arthur Spingarn: "Some day I hope to be freer than I am at present, so that administrative detail will not get in the way of more serious scholarship."[24]

At the same time that the situation at Wilberforce was improving, Wesley was approached by several members of the Fisk University alumni to allow his name to be placed in nomination for the Fisk presidency. Although Wesley was honored by the call of his alma mater, he believed there was little justification at that time to leave Wilberforce. Furthermore, he was fairly confident that the alumni would not be able to impose a candidate at Fisk. He rejected the idea of having the alumni present his name. However, when they were polled for a favorite candidate, Wesley was their choice.

Wesley expressed his feelings regarding the campaign process in his relationship to Wilberforce when he said:

> For I realize that if our efforts should fail, I would be in a particularly embarrassing position with reference to the University clientele, that is, I would have to

26

make myself satisfied at Wilberforce now that I could not go to Fisk. That was the dangerous part of this whole matter so far as my immediate career was concerned, though I felt that I would be able to carry through this program [Wilberforce] after this kind of result.[25]

Wesley's energies soon were returned in full to the administration of Wilberforce where the situation was again in a state of flux. An official statement by the North Central Association of Colleges and Secondary Schools Board of Review had sparked a controversy between President Wesley and Bishop Ransom. The board had said, "The members of the Board, as individuals considered your [Dr. Wesley's] leadership in the institution the single point of strength that would warrant continuation of accreditation for the coming year."[26] Nevertheless, Bishop Ransom accused Wesley of having contributed to the eventual loss of accreditation that occurred in 1947, and held him responsible for the "twenty points of weakness" for which the North Central Association had cited Wilberforce. Among these were the hiring of inexperienced and immature teachers and the excessive number of relatives employed on the campus.

In truth, the issue of relatives employed on campus was important to the Wesley-Ransom feud, but in quite a different way than is implied in the official documents. Insiders had long felt that a third person—Bishop Ransom's wife, Georgia M. Teal Ransom—was to blame for the growing split between the two men. This may, in fact, have been the case. Prior to her marriage to the bishop, she had served Wilberforce as dean of women. In 1944, she was fired by President Wesley ostensibly over a "severe clash of ideas."

In any case, Wesley denied the charges made by Ransom as "collections of incorrections, exaggerations and untruths." He also called upon him to step down from the board in order not to impede further developments at Wilberforce.[27] In response, the church board met on June 9, 1947, and dismissed Charles Wesley as president of Wilberforce by a vote of sixteen to five. There was an attempt by the church to make concessions by offering Wesley one year's pay if he resigned, but he refused. Dr. Charles Leander Hill was named to replace Wesley.

At the commencement exercises the next day, Wesley called upon friends, faculty, and students to join him in developing a state-supported College of Education and Industrial Arts, free from any connection with the church. The state board endorsed Wesley's action by a six to three vote and called Wesley's dismissal a "breach of agreement" between the church and state boards operating as the Joint Executive Committee. The church filed an injunction to prevent Wesley from using the university's property and supplies.

The case of the church versus Wesley was heard on August 5, 1947. An attempt by the church board to withdraw their complaint and have the case dismissed without prejudice was denied due to the defendant's objections. The injunction forbidding Wesley to act as president of Wilberforce was upheld, but the court noted that the real issue in the case—whether or not Wesley could act as president of the state-run college within the university—was not before the court for decision. Wesley was asked to file a statement on that issue. Until that time the court dissolved "the temporary restraining order insofar as it would prevent Dr. Wesley from acting as president of the College of Education and Industrial Arts at Wilberforce University."

On June 16, 1947, seven days after Wesley was ousted from Wilberforce, he accepted the presidency of Morgan State College, where he had been the unanimous choice of the Board of Trustees. However, Wesley did not serve in the position because he was unwilling to leave Wilberforce without "stabiliz[ing] the work of this college as against the group of persons who have neither the desire nor the purpose to maintain a first rate educational institution but rather to continue a stage on which they may exploit their political ambition in the future as in the past."[28]

By September 9, the split had widened to include the state board of trustees as well. In accordance with state law, eight of the nine board members were to be appointed by the governor of Ohio and the one remaining member by the AME church. The church declined to seat any board member, citing the strained relations between the church and the state as their reason. A second member—Joseph Gomez, appointed by Governor Herbert but an AME minister as well—refused his appointment.

On that same day, Judge Frank L. Johnson of the common pleas court gave legal sanction to the Wilberforce University split, ruling that the state was entitled to operate its own college at Wilberforce. The judge further stated, "There was very little, if any, evidence in the record that Dr. Wesley ever attempted, after his discharge from the Wilberforce presidency, to act as president of Wilberforce University." In the judge's opinion "it is too late for them [the church leaders] to complain that the state cannot operate the college of education and industrial arts after the state has spent thousands of dollars on buildings and equipment and support for the school."[29] Regarding the physical facilities of the (now) two schools, Judge Johnson decreed that the state should use none of the church's property, nor the church any of the state's property until such time as "they can agree upon an interchange . . . which they had been doing over a long period of years and which it seems to the court that they could now do."

The judge clearly felt that another issue in the case was really much ado about nothing—the church's charge that invitations sent out by the senior class of the state-controlled departments had illegally stated that the 1947 summer commencement exercises would be held under the auspices of Wilberforce University. He said that it was "generally recognized" that the issuance of such invitations is an action taken by the students, not by officers of the college.

Finally, concerning the proper name to be used for the state school—a matter around which much of the courtroom argument had revolved—Judge Johnson ordered that the state college "drop the words 'at Wilberforce University,' and only use the title, 'College of Education and Industrial Arts at Wilberforce, Greene County, Ohio.'"[30]

Thus, as students were arriving to begin the 1947–48 school year, the schools that had been joined became separate. The College of Education and Industrial Arts at Wilberforce, commonly referred to thereafter as Wilberforce State College, opened with an enrollment of 966 students and 97 faculty members. Wilberforce University's enrollment was approximately 400, with a faculty of 47. The state school also had the more substantial opening budget—$581,784 as compared to Wilberforce University's $364,000.

After Wesley vacated his university office, the students placed a sign on the president's door which read, "No Wesley—No Students [,] No Students—No School." Although classes at Wilberforce University continued on schedule, many disgruntled students' views on the Wesley affairs were reported in the *Ohio State News*. Thomas Sanchez, a freshman from Texas, remarked, "The Church is unfair to Dr. Wesley . . . he represented the students." Another student, responding to a minister's statement that "God is in our fight," retorted, "God ain't got a penny. The State of Ohio has plenty of money and can run the school better."[31]

Despite the 1947 court ruling, the conflict was not entirely resolved. Although building and renovation of the state-supported department continued apace (five major building projects were completed in 1949), it was clearly not a separate entity to the extent that Ohio's other interracial public colleges were. Thus, in January 1951, Norman L. McGhee, a Cleveland lawyer serving on the school's board of trustees, proposed in an open letter to Senator Albert L. Daniels that the state should discontinue operations and sell its physical property or, alternatively, should reconstitute the operations of the school so that it was unequivocally interracial. In McGhee's words:

> If it is found that other state-supported institutions are not adequate to meet the educational needs of the youth of the state, then I urge that interests of the entire citizenry of Ohio would be served best by enactment of legislation that would direct its complete reorganization as a state-supported school requiring its operation on a definite inter-racial basis as to administrative officers, trustees, faculty and student body similar to all other state-supported colleges.
>
> In this way, and in this way only, can the idea be dispelled that the separate maintenance of the college of education and industrial arts at Wilberforce will be other than a "Jim Crow" school supported and maintained by the state to the everlasting shame of a vast number of its right thinking and democratic loving citizens.[32]

In April 1951, McGhee's proposals appeared to be reaching fruition when the Ohio House and Senate at last concurred on a bill to change the school's name to Central State College and to put it on an equal footing with other public colleges in Ohio by permitting it to award Bachelor of Arts degrees. The bill additionally reduced the number of trustees from nine to seven and permitted the college to appoint its own business manager. An amendment to empower the governor to appoint an entirely new board of trustees upon enactment of the bill was defeated. However, Governor Frank J. Lausche invoked his veto power to halt this bill. In the message to the legislature accompanying his veto Governor Lausche explained:

> The State of Ohio went to Wilberforce University (in 1887) not as a rival and competitor but as a friend with the purpose of cooperating through mutual agreement. It was never intended that the State of Ohio should become a competitor of Wilberforce University. It was the purpose of the state not to harm Wilberforce in its operation as a private institution. . . . The result of this bill would be to definitely create a situation of competition which, in the end, may bring destruction of the life of Wilberforce University. . . . It is further my belief that if the bill becomes law, the state will find itself confronted with the charge that it is operating a segregated school.[33]

This fear of charges of willful segregation probably had arisen because the state school had outpaced the church school in enrollment, largely through the recruitment of half of that enrollment from outside Ohio. Yet it had few more white students in 1951 than it had ever had. Nevertheless, in the second week of May, the legislature—much to the approval of The Central State College students—voted to override the governor's veto.[34]

During the turbulent years between 1947 and 1951, Charles Wesley remained at the helm of Central State, doing his best to smooth its course for the benefit of students and faculty. He may have recalled as he worked a letter from W. E. B. Du Bois in 1932. Du Bois had predicted:

> Wilberforce if properly conducted has an extraordinary opportunity. It can become practically a State University; it has a beautiful location and a strategic [sic] one in the center of the United States. It is worth saving, but its salvation will be the death of many a good and self-sacrificing man.[35]

Charles Wesley, just such a "good and sacrificing man," did not die as a result of his service, but he must sometimes have had serious concerns as he gazed out his office window at the ravine that, symbolically and literally, divided the two halves of the campus. In his reestablished, and now independent institution, Wesley's goal was to build a first rate college, and he would attempt to do so during a period of unprecedented growth and change in the nature of American higher education.

three

Expansion Period, 1951·1965

Although the institution evolved continuously from its establishment in 1887, 1951 marked a major watershed in its history, for it was in that year that it began using the title Central State College. During the period 1951 to 1965, the year in which it achieved university status and Dr. Wesley resigned his presidency, Central State experienced a period of exceptional growth and development. Not only did it expand its physical facilities and operating expenditures to meet the needs of a continuously rising student enrollment and a corresponding enlargement of its faculty and administration, but it advanced as well in less tangible, but even more important ways. It also faced and overcame a period of financial instability and charges of discriminatory and irresponsible policies.

There are several reasons for Central State's growth during these years. One reason, of course, was the nationwide increase in college attendance encouraged by the growing availability of money from the state and federal governments to supplement student fees and other private revenue sources. But other factors, peculiar to Central State, were also at work. First, Central State held an attractive position as a predominantly black, small-town college in a northern state. Second, it maintained, partly through its earlier affiliation with the African Methodist Episcopal Church, a reputation for a highly moral and religious campus environment. And finally, the character of the school's long-time president, Charles Wesley, contributed greatly to its advancement. He served the school directly through his farsightedness and his forceful leadership, and indirectly through the recognition that his personal scholarship brought to Central State.

Before detailing these factors in Central State's development, it may be useful to examine some statistics and examples of that development during the 1951–65 period. The most obvious expansion was in enrollment. In 1951, Central State's enrollment stood at 790 students. It rose to 947 in 1955, to 1,743 in 1960, and to 2,241 in 1965.[1] The increase over these fifteen years—276 percent—compares favorably with the growth pattern at public colleges in Ohio and elsewhere in the United States. But this rapid rise in numbers was not indicative of a disregard for quality. President Wesley's 1956 report to the board of trustees notes with pride that Central State is "obtaining a larger number of students . . . who stand at, or near the top of their respective graduating classes."

Two programs instituted in the mid-1950s may be largely credited for this improvement. In 1956, Walter G. Sellers, the director of student recruiting, began a policy of encouraging prospective students to apply for admission at the completion of their seventh semester's high school work, and of awarding provisional acceptance permits to those who followed this procedure. This policy made Central State more competitive among Ohio public colleges, and with institutions in other states as well.

Second, in 1956, Central State's board of trustees approved a project using the College Testing Service for prerequisite testing of incoming students. This provided the school's faculty and staff with general information needed for program planning as well as individual data needed for counseling and remediation.

While the student body grew in size and quality, the college's physical facilities could not always keep pace—a situation similar to that at other schools throughout the nation. However, every effort was made to accommodate the crowding without a reduction in the quality of education. Among these accommodations were the introduction of a large lecture format coupled with smaller discussion sections in certain subject areas, and an extension of class meeting hours throughout the day and on Saturday.

While Central State's enrollment was constantly increasing during the 1951–65 period, the size of its faculty did not always grow proportionately. In 1951, there were eighty-nine faculty members: thirty-two professors; twelve associate professors; fifteen assistant professors; twenty-one instructors; and nine assistant instructors. Fourteen faculty members possessed doctoral degrees, and two others were near completion of this degree.

By 1965, the faculty size had increased only to 101 members, but more significant advances were made in the quality of these teachers. In 1965,

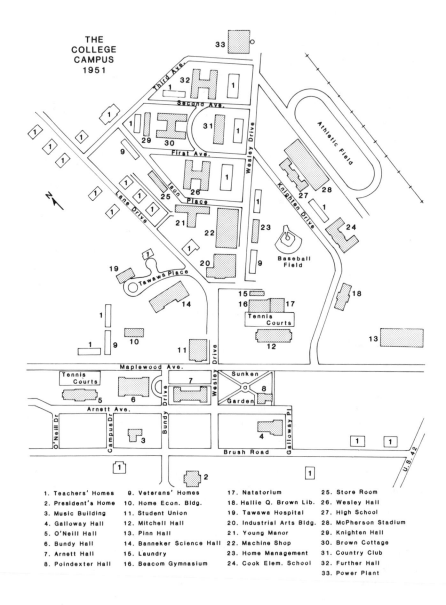

THE
COLLEGE
CAMPUS
1951

1. Teachers' Homes	9. Veterans' Homes	17. Natatorium	25. Store Room
2. President's Home	10. Home Econ. Bldg.	18. Hallie Q. Brown Lib.	26. Wesley Hall
3. Music Building	11. Student Union	19. Tawawa Hospital	27. High School
4. Galloway Hall	12. Mitchell Hall	20. Industrial Arts Bldg.	28. McPherson Stadium
5. O'Neill Hall	13. Pinn Hall	21. Young Manor	29. Knighten Hall
6. Bundy Hall	14. Banneker Science Hall	22. Machine Shop	30. Brown Cottage
7. Arnett Hall	15. Laundry	23. Home Management	31. Country Club
8. Poindexter Hall	16. Beacom Gymnasium	24. Cook Elem. School	32. Further Hall
			33. Power Plant

the year that Central State became a university, it employed twenty-five professors, twenty-four associate professors, fifteen assistant professors, twenty-eight instructors, and four assistant instructors. The number of faculty with Ph.D.'s had risen to thirty-nine.

One reason for these improvements was that the salaries of Central State's instructional staff were brought into line with those at other state-supported schools in Ohio. For the 1959–60 academic year, the average salary for all ranks at the other five state colleges totaled $7,624, while the average salary at Central State was only $6,593—a difference of $1,031. In the following academic year, however, this difference had been reduced substantially to a margin of only $55. President Wesley also noted in reporting this improvement to *The Gold Torch* that these 1960–61 salary figures compared favorably with others across the country, according to the American Association of University Professors' Self-Grading Scale.

Additionally, faculty hiring practices during these years became more selective. Central State sought out experienced scholars from other institutions in this country and abroad, and appointed younger teachers whose academic records showed promise of outstanding achievement in both teaching and research. The school also began promoting outstanding teachers from its own staff to administrative positions at correspondingly higher rates of compensation.

Not only did across-the-board salary adjustments make it possible for Central State to acquire and maintain highly qualified faculty, but a system of merit increases, awarded to those distinguishing themselves in scholarly productions, assured that these faculty members maintained the intellectual output of which they were capable. Howard H. Long, dean of the college, discussed merit increases in a 1954 letter to James T. Henry, chairman of the Committee on Future Planning:

> The College must stimulate scholarly productions by faculty members who are properly equipped and of research temperament, and reward those who produce in some measure commensurate with the importance of their production. An institution of higher learning is essentially a community of scholars, but even scholars need the stimulus of financial and status rewards.

Accordingly, a merit system of promotions was established in 1954.

Methods for monitoring the quality of instruction were also put in place during the expansion years. Mindful that an emphasis on research can lead to neglect of basic teaching duties, Dean Long joined the deans of

Ohio's other state colleges in 1954 in suggesting "More and more we shall have to go to students with various instruments of evaluation as a major factor in evaluating the program of the college, if we wish to avoid a deluge of wishful thinking [regarding curriculum planning]."[2] Thus, student evaluation of faculty was begun in 1959, and in December 1960 the Board of Trustees instituted a policy of systematic objective evaluations for all teachers.

The family-like environment at Central State, an unquestioned good for the students, led ultimately to practices which had negative as well as positive effects. One was the desire to keep internal dissent from surfacing, and the other was the custom of self-sacrifice for the welfare of others—usually of the faculty and staff for the needs of the students. In the minuses as well as the pluses, the hand of Charles Wesley can readily be seen.

Harry G. Johns, who served as comptroller, business manager, and vice president for fiscal affairs at the school from 1949 to 1965, remarks, "As chief administrators and members of his [Wesley's] cabinet we were not permitted to utter the word 'can't' in his presence, no matter how difficult or impossible, at the moment, the project might seem."[3] Though Wesley's life and work show him to be a practical man as well as an idealist, he seems more often to have shown the idealistic side to those who served under him. While he would honestly assess the possible obstacles, he refused to acknowledge that these might ever remain insurmountable.

One prime example of this was the decision in the early 1960s to begin offering graduate degrees at Central State. The designation of the school as a university was preceded by accreditation for the program of graduate study by the North Central Association. Early in 1963, Arthur D. Pickett, associate director of the honors programs at the University of Illinois in Chicago, was assigned by the association to act as a liaison, helping Central State to prepare their program in such a way as to ensure ultimate accreditation. Pickett made several visits to the campus conducting interviews similar to those which would eventually be conducted by the association's evaluating team. Then he provided the school with feedback, questions, and recommendations as the proposed program took shape.

In an official follow-up letter to his visit of May 23–24, 1963, Pickett wrote to Wesley:

> There is no question but what the president is strongly in favor of the graduate effort. He is undoubtedly the prime mover as he well should be. His impetus has

gone far to influence his faculty, for by and large they respect his judgement and honor his interest in them and the College. In group meetings the faculty seems to be agreed in the necessity for early development of graduate offerings. During single interviews the responses are more negative.[4]

He goes on to cite concerns with staff inadequacy, prematurity of the effort, lack of necessary organization, and fear of predominance by the Education Department (the first of two departments scheduled to offer the advanced degree)—none of which had been expressed during the combined faculty-administration meeting.

Perhaps even more revealing is Wesley's reply to Pickett—a reply which remained unsent in his office files and was replaced by a somewhat less emotional response. Wesley's original answer to Pickett's letter states:

> The Board of Trustees has discussed this subject again and again through my presentation, and finally a resolution was approved *unanimously* for the presentation of the subject of graduate study to the faculty for discussion. The faculty *unanimously*—with the individuals whom you mentioned present and voting—approved a resolution for this purpose with two committees appointed—(1) Education Policy and (2) Faculty Research and Graduate Study. The resolution was approved *unanimously* for a second time at the last faculty meeting for the academic year 1962. Again at the first meeting of the academic year, 1962-63, September 13, 1962, there was the same approval and also approval for the transition from "college" to "university."[5]

The emphatic tone of the letter, even more than its content, displays Wesley's irritation that these faculty members should have violated the confidentiality of the "family," after having acquiesced with their vote to his plan, by telling Pickett, an outsider, of their doubts.

Indeed, Paul McStallworth, a former professor of history, remembers just this quality in Wesley's leadership style. "He was," according to McStallworth, "adamant against personal criticism of his role in public but would accept it with great objectivity in private." Harry Johns concurs: "This is not to say that he did not listen and take advice from those who disagreed with him. It is to say, however, that once he had made a decision on a particular course of action, as a member of the team, you were expected to move with dispatch in carrying out your responsibilities within that decision." Wesley's methods certainly did not appeal to everyone, and "the submission of a resignation was seldom given the right of recall or revocation." But his methods did prove to be what was best for

Central State at the time and under the particular conditions of his presidency.

Another of Wesley's convictions—that the students' welfare must always be the top priority of the school—also produced mixed results. Johns states that "the president also believed that no student who desired an education should be denied the opportunity solely on the basis that he or she could not meet the financial cost." In this period, prior to the initiation of the many types of government assistance which later became available, the burden of finding alternative funding generally fell to the student. At Central State this was often not the case; the school itself undertook the task. Certainly, traditional forms of financial aid were used and an extensive work study program was devised to cover many more students. But at a school whose student body was drawn so heavily from rural and inner city poor families, these methods were not enough to help all students in need. Johns suggests that "many innovative ways were worked out to assist students in their quest for a college degree," though he does not specify what they were.

Mildred Henderson, a longtime staff member, also recalls the frequent problem of needy students. When asked by interviewer Joseph D. Lewis, an associate professor of history, "How did students handle financial problems without work study?" Ms. Henderson replied simply, "Dr. Wesley would let them in school." And often the solution, in fact, was just as simple as the recounting of it suggests. If sufficient funds could not be procured, the students' papers were merely processed as if they had been, and their education proceeded. Walter Sellers, Director of University Relations and Alumni Affairs, who was part of the Wesley administration for fourteen years, states:

> This good-heartedness caused Dr. Wesley and the university some problems in the latter years of his administration since he did permit a number of students to register and pursue their education without having paid the required basic fees.
>
> Dr. Wesley ran into this situation because he felt that we were dealing with first generation college students, and if given the opportunity, eventually they would repay the state and the nation more than had been invested in them.

Obviously if this type of financial sustenance were to be given to any significant number of students, money would have to be cut from other segments of the budget. The need for extensive building and repair on the physical plant, as well as the state's close monitoring of capital funds meant that little could be saved in these areas. Thus operating expenses must have been diverted. Supplies might have been reduced somewhat, but the largest and therefore the most likely budget area for the cuts was in salaries.

McStallworth cautiously states that "faculty appropriations were allegedly on some occasions shared to help deserving poor needy students. . . . It is strongly alleged the fiscal situation was aggravated with the allocations of funds to aid students which [should] have been for faculty and other services." Though there is, of course, no verifiable evidence of this, it is hinted at by so many former faculty members and administrators that the case for its being true is a strong one. It might be argued that this diversion of funds from faculty to students was not a matter of sacrifice at all since they did not directly give money earmarked for them. Yet there is no record of faculty members protesting or attempting to stop this practice. Surely among such a closely knit group it could have been no secret. Two other reports, one by long-time Professor Leonora C. Lane and another by Pickett, suggest that faculty members who knew of these gifts to students probably agreed with their necessity. They often showed themselves willing to make other types of personal sacrifices for the young people entrusted to their care. Dr. Lane speaks of her own work and that of her husband:

> I was married to the former Director of Athletics in this school; one talent with the Athletics Department, they never seem to have enough money but you learn to live without it. Mr. Lane had to get students up and on a train by 4:00 a.m. I never knew the Athletic Department to miss a train. So I had to get them up and knock on their doors. This is something I think you [the students assembled to hear this interview] should know about in order to build a good sturdy respect for our teachers; the teachers who work with us stay here. The people we had did not work for money only.[6]

Even someone only superficially connected with the school could observe this trait as well. Pickett, in his address to the faculty on May 23, 1963, cautioned against proceeding with a graduate program if it meant using monies or faculty time drawn from the undergraduate program. Pickett warned, "The teaching faculty may share its instruction with the undergraduate college, but it must do so on a released time basis, which is to say that graduate instruction should not be added to the present load of any instructor. Even if the instructor volunteers or wishes it so, this should not occur."[7] That Pickett should have developed, during such a short association with them, the impression that members of the Central State faculty would be willing to assume these additional duties is a strong indicator that the willingness to sacrifice must have been a pervasive feature of campus life.

To what extent did the students, who were the beneficiaries of all this care and devotion, reciprocate or acknowledge their debts? Not to the full extent, certainly. McStallworth complains that there are many who were aided by Central State who "should have long ago acknowledged their thanks and appreciation by repayments, payments of pledges, financial gifts and bequeaths to Central." But then many children are lax in expressing gratitude for their parents' sacrifices for them. Many others, as can be seen from records of alumni support, have returned to help the university as they were helped by it.

In addition to upgrading students and faculty, Central State sought to better its programs. Two seemingly minor additions, an annual Career Day and an Honors Day celebration, illustrate the importance of the college's attention to detail in providing the best possible atmosphere for learning. Begun in 1956, Career Day was an opportunity for students to obtain information about occupational trends, prospective starting salaries, opportunities for advancement, and the advantages and disadvantages of a given career choice. Resource persons to conduct seminars were sought out not only by divisional directors of the various disciplines, but by students themselves, thus giving the student planners of Career Day even more contact with the world of work. The pragmatic issues aired at a Career Day conference could have such objective benefits as a higher rate of post-graduate placements within the student's field of study, as well as such intangibles as greater job satisfaction.

The goal of Honors Day, on the other hand, was not to better the students' lives after graduation, but to provide them with rewards and recognition during their stay at college. Held each spring, beginning in 1953, this awards celebration gave the college an opportunity to display its regard for high academic achievement. In addition to special honors given to those who excelled in a certain area of study, those who had been on the Dean's List during the year received a more formal commendation from the school. Later, in 1957, the Honors Committee's responsibilities were expanded to include a body of honors courses (actually individualized minor research) to be offered by some departments. The Honors Program not only provided incentive for those students capable of outstanding performance, but served to create appropriate role models for all students.

A program far more essential than these two, and integral to the day-to-day life of Central State, was the program for remedial instruction in

English and math skills. Since, in spite of prerequisite testing, a distressing number of Central State students came to the campus incompletely prepared for the demands of college-level work, laboratory classes for freshmen were initiated in 1950. Originally, these laboratories offered only basic instruction in such things as grammar, spelling, reading comprehension, and elementary mathematics. They were conducted separately from required freshman English and mathematics courses, and they earned the students no credit toward graduation. However, in the mid-1950s, alterations were undertaken to make the program both more appealing and more accessible to the students. The freshman English courses required in the curriculum (Communication 101 and 102) were extended from three hours to four, but regularly scheduled attendance in laboratory was made mandatory. Second, additions were made to the remedial program itself to include an orientation to the tools of culture which are necessary to the mastery of advanced work. Finally, in 1960, study skills work was taken up by the reading laboratory, and other parts of the remedial program were once again upgraded.

Although utilized by a smaller clientele, another offshoot of the remedial program, a workshop for foreign students, proved to be equally successful. In these weekly workshops, students from other countries were given an opportunity both to sharpen their language skills and, in some cases, to become acquainted with western culture. American students also benefited when they were invited to attend as peer tutors.

However, not all of Central State's efforts to improve its programs were directed toward those students with specialized talents or needs. Curriculum development was an ongoing effort throughout the college. A 1957 issue of *The Gold Torch* looked back on a decade of progress and made the following observations. In 1947, the College of Education and Industrial Arts (Wilberforce), without accreditation, awarded two degrees. Its successor, Central State, had national, state, and regional accreditation, and granted four degrees. Just five years later, in 1962, Central State petitioned the Ohio legislature for university status, initiated some limited offerings of graduate degrees, and began broadening its available courses of study in anticipation of university designation. Finally, in 1965, the dream became reality: Central State College became Central State University.

Although the advancement of an institution for higher education must first come from its personnel and from its program, it cannot maintain for long the quality of learning without adequate physical facilities. In this respect, too, Central State expanded during the years under discussion.

O'Neill Hall (1890), named in honor of the late State Senator John O'Neill, was a four-story and ground brick dormitory. The building accommodated about one hundred and twenty students and was used primarily for freshman women. (Destroyed by tornado.)

From 1947 to 1957, Central State had more than doubled its land holdings—from 200 to 558 acres. Thus, when enrollment began its sharp rise in the mid-1950s, plenty of space was available for expansion.

Major renovation and reconstruction projects were done on existing buildings, including O'Neil Hall, Arnett Hall, Mitchell Hall, Bundy Hall, Galloway Hall, Jenkins Hall (the old student union), Lee Hall (the Teacher Education Building), Young Hall, Stadium Hall, the original Hallie Q. Brown Library (converted to a music building), Cook Elementary School (converted to become the Home Economics Laboratory), the Natatorium, and two private residences, which became the Alumni House and the Guest House. Many new buildings were also erected or purchased: Robert Shauter Hall (1952), Homewood Cottage (1952), the fire house (1954), Hughes Hall (1954), a cafeteria (1958), Jane E. Hunter Hall (1958), Page Hall (1959), Broaddus Hall (1959), Lucinda Cook Laboratory School (1960), the new Hallie Q. Brown Library (1959), Beacon Gymnasium II (1961), and a new College Union (1964). Maintenance buildings, power plants, and sewage systems were, of course, comparably upgraded to keep pace with building.

The availability of financial support necessary for growth was a major factor influencing Central State during the expansion years. State and federal government spending for higher education rose rapidly during the 1951–65 period. At the federal level, the increases resulted largely from the influx of World War II and Korean War veterans, and later from the emphasis during the Kennedy and Johnson administrations on social welfare and education programs. In the 1950–51 federal budget, $2,550,640,000 was appropriated for education. This appropriation had increased by approximately 25 percent, to $3,181,397,000, by 1965. However, the proportion of this total going to higher education increased far more rapidly, from $304,111 in 1951 to $925,503,000 in 1965—a rise of over 300 percent.[8]

State appropriations were similarly on the upswing throughout the period under discussion. In the 1951–53 biennium, the General Assembly of the State of Ohio allocated $2,465,200 for capital improvements at its six state colleges and universities. By the 1965–67 biennium, this figure had reached $164,620,466, a leap of approximately 6,000 percent (though this sum was, in 1965, to be divided among eleven state-assisted institutions). Despite the fact that Central State's share of these capital improvement dollars was small, percentage of increase for the university was a dramatic 3,300 percent—growing from $117,500 in 1951–53 to $3,922,000 in 1965–67.

Ohio appropriations for operating expenses also rose 332 percent, from $21,481,335 in 1951–52 to $71,239,750 in 1965–66. However, this total figure actually represents a decrease in the amount of money received for each full-time equivalent (FTE) student. As enrollment across the state grew, the full-time equivalent appropriation dropped from $1,068 in 1951–52 to $829 in 1965–66.

In the opinion of Wesley and other Central State administrators, this system resulted in an unfair distribution of funding, particularly for

The original Hallie Q. Brown Library (1948), named in honor of Dr. Hallie Q. Brown, Class of 1873, was a two-story brick structure erected through the cooperation of the Federal Works Agency, Washington, D.C., and the State of Ohio. It had been constructed to provide adequate library facilities, including a reading room, a reserve book room, offices, work rooms, staff lounge, a bindery and the Hallie Q. Brown Memorial room. Open shelves made a large number of volumes available to readers.

Arnett Hall (1901), named in honor of the late Benjamin W. Arnett, provided dormitory facilities for approximately one hundred students. The hall had been completely redecorated and modernized, with guest parlors on the first floor. This hall was used mainly for sophomore and junior women, and later it housed administrative offices. (Destroyed by tornado.)

Mitchell Hall (1910), named in honor of the late Samuel T. Mitchell, former President, was an attractive building of colonial style, housing about seventy senior women. A cafeteria and a recreational room were in the basement. (Razed in early 1970s.)

The Health Service, Lackey Health Center (Tawawa Hospital) (1927), named in honor of Dr. Harry Lackey, was a two-story brick building erected by students enrolled in courses in building construction. It contained ward rooms, a laboratory, and a dispensary. (Destroyed by tornado.)

Bundy Hall (1917), named in honor of the late Reverend Charles Bundy, a member of the state Board of Trustees, housed the administration offices, including the offices of the President, the Dean of the College, the Business Manager, the Bursar, the Registrar, and the Personnel Department; and classrooms and lecture rooms for the Division of Business and Economics and the Division of Education. (Destroyed by tornado.)

Scarborough House (1908), the home of Central State's presidents, was built by students in the carpentry classes. This house was listed in the National Register of Historic Places by the National Park Service of the United States Department of Interior. (Destroyed by tornado.)

Poindexter Hall (1905), named in honor of the late Reverend James Poindexter, a member of the state Board of Trustees. This building was occupied by the Department of Music and the second-floor was occupied by the Department of Arts and Art Education. (Razed in early 1970s.)

Industrial Arts Education Building (1917) was a one-story brick and concrete structure erected mainly through the work of students. The offices of the Division of Industrial and Technical Education, general shop, machine shop and laboratories for auto mechanics, carpentry and woodworking, metal work, forging, electricity, aeronautics, and the Printing Department was located in this building. (Destroyed by tornado.)

Benjamin F. Lee Education Building, the Teacher Education Building (1925), was a two-story building complete with modern equipment, classrooms and laboratories for instruction in the education of teachers. (Destroyed by tornado.)

Homewood Cottage (early 1900s) was a faculty and staff housing unit. (Razed during 1960s.)

Jenkins Hall (1880), the oldest building on campus, had housed the veterans' office, the bookstore, radio station, campus security, audio-visual aids, CSU Federal Credit Union, and the College Grille. (Destroyed by tornado.)

Stadium Hall (1920) served as a dressing room and equipment room for athletes performing at McPherson Stadium and later, a receiving depot for university supplies and equipment. (Razed during the 1970s.)

Beacon Gymnasium (1919) the main center for sports and social gathering during the early years of C.S.U. (Destroyed by fire in early 1970s.)

Galloway Hall (1906) housed faculty offices, classrooms and main auditorium. (Destroyed by tornado.)

schools that came into the state system later and that, like Central State, had inadequate and deteriorating physical facilities. Responding to a 1965 board of regents report which addressed the image problem of Central State as a "colored school," Wesley said, "A lot of members of the General Assembly also need to reorient their thinking along lines of financial support. It's a mistake to appropriate money on the basis of enrollment, anyway."[9]

While this system of funding was widely criticized, both for these reasons and for its effect on class size and student-teacher ratios, there is no doubt that it provided a major impetus to Central State and other state schools to increase their enrollments and to seek alternative funding for such correlative facilities as dormitories that could not be funded by the state.

For Ohio colleges that were able to attract a steadily expanding number of students, the gains in funding were large. At Central State the amount of state-appropriated operating dollars more than doubled in the fifteen-year period, from $843,000 in 1951–52 to $1,858,000 in 1965–66. Nevertheless, when these dollars are divided by the number of FTE enrollments (which increased from 790 in 1951–52 to 2,241 in 1965–66), they show a decline of about 1.5 percent per year for each FTE student. Thus Central State was placed in a paradoxical situation. The societal need for more college berths had opportunely coincided with a political climate favorable to government support of higher education. However, funding was always being outpaced by enrollment growth. This, coupled with the time lag inevitable in capital improvement projects, resulted in a great deal of stress on both human and physical resources during Central State's expansion years.

Part of Central State's solution to this problem was to increase the portion of student costs actually paid by the students. To this end, undergraduate student fees were raised from $173 in 1951–52 to $400 in 1965–66—or 231 percent. The nonresident surcharges for the same years were $90 and $370, respectively—a 411 percent jump. Mindful of the burden these rising fees presented to the individual student, the school's administrators also sought solutions through financial aid programs and creative management of available funds.

In addition to the various scholarship and loan programs offered to students, Central State maintained during this period an outstanding student employment system. A large majority of those who applied were placed on the college payroll at salaries high enough to defray rising student fees considerably.[10] The school was able to employ so many students because of its self-sufficiency of physical operation and its community service. To cite just a few examples, Central State's library repaired and rebound its own damaged books and bound its own periodicals by hand. Not only did this result in significant savings in the library budget, but it provided additional openings for student workers with some industrial arts skills. Similarly, the college-operated Children's Center, while providing educational and recreational opportunities for local youngsters, served as a source of revenue for Central State and a placement facility for student workers skilled in child care.

The most unique of Central State's self-sufficiency programs, however, emanated from their Department of Agriculture. In addition to its function as a learning laboratory, the college farm produced poultry, fish, meat, and dairy products to be consumed in Arnett Cafeteria and the College Grille and to be sold through local markets. The benefits of this program could be counted in savings in the school's food budget and in revenue, as well as in employment opportunities for students.

In order for these student assistance programs to have a maximum impact on the decisions of high school students about to select a college, Central State's Committee on Scholarship and Student Aid, beginning in 1956, prepared and distributed a pamphlet entitled "Financing an Education at Central State College." This unusually complete booklet gave detailed information about all phases of the student aid program, including "payment of bills, R.O.T.C., scholarships, loans, grants in aid, cadet teachers, . . . and problems of student aid peculiar to athletes."

While the general social and economic atmosphere favoring growth of higher education certainly was a force in Central State's expansion, other factors, pertaining to the college exclusively, were also at work. First, Central State grew because it held a unique position in the northern part of the United States. There were simply not many small-town, predominantly black institutions that were respected in the North. More importantly though, Central State was consistently able to recognize and provide for the special backgrounds, needs, and interests of black students, while also establishing Central State as a good college, rather than a good black college.

Another point of attraction, easily overlooked, was Central State's rural environment. Located in the agricultural southwestern corner of Ohio, yet within convenient travel distance from Dayton, Cincinnati, and Columbus, Central State provided its students and faculty with the protective isolation of the typical "college town." Indeed, a 1958 article from the student newspaper, *The Gold Torch,* refers to the school as "undisturbed by the distractions of an urban center." The paper goes on to praise its "approximately five hundred acres . . . of natural beauty," and concludes, "The campus walks and drives, bordered by trees, shrubbery, ivy-covered buildings and the sunken garden provide an atmosphere of beauty, serenity and dignity."

While such surroundings are generally attractive to both college-bound students and their parents (and often to prospective faculty members as well), a statement by President Wesley in his 1956 report to the board of trustees underscored the special importance of this environment to a school with a predominantly black enrollment seeking to integrate and broaden its appeal:

> In these days of integration this college is moving as rapidly as it can from exclusive Negro enrollment to an integrated enrollment in both faculty and student body. This development cannot be pushed with any artificial motivation. It will come slowly in this area but we believe with certainty. Our main purpose now should be to announce this declaration and to have it well known so that all those who are qualified and desire to come can feel free to do so. Closely associated with this announcement is the determination to build a first rate college which will compare favorably with other colleges and *not to conduct a college which is typical of the neighborhoods in which Negroes live in some of our larger urban areas.*[11]

Wesley is candid here in his admission that full integration will come slowly to Central State. More importantly, he reminds the board that a predominance of qualities drawn from urban black community life will be detrimental to the college. This is typical of his frank assessment of racial issues. He, and the college he headed, never lost sight of the fact that many students who matriculated at Central State during the 1951–65 period were less well prepared for college life than the average college freshman.

For example, in his statement to the Faculty Institute in 1960, he stated:

> Each of the three groups among us (faculty, administrators, and students) is also interested, I hope, in the mental health of our students. Some of them come from broken homes, from parents who are themselves defeated or frustrated by race, family, economic, social and community pressures. Here in these four years these students must learn to achieve a new mental health for themselves and to take it home with them.

Central State University

A similar sentiment was expressed by Howard H. Long, the dean of the college, in response to the request of the Faculty Committee on Planning for the years 1954 to 1965:

> Central State College should seek to meet the residual needs of its students; that is to say, we shall have to emphasize what for them is left insufficiently emphasized or provided for by the communities and by the homes from which they come. Central State College has a tremendous opportunity to make a contribution in providing for students who have been deprived of standard educational and socioeconomic opportunities. It is somewhat strange that colleges similarly situated have not heretofore either clearly conceived or sensibly provided on the basis of research and tested experience, adequate programs implied by the residual needs of their students.[12]

Thus Central State set its course to improve its students' chances of academic success and thus to improve the quality of American life in general and the lives of black Americans in particular. Although these goals were significant to Central State's period of expansion, more significant still were the campus policies based upon these goals.

One illustration of the college's supportive attitude toward its students may be found in its "Guide Book for Freshmen and New Students, 1957–58." In addition to the standard information about registration procedures, orientation dates, and housing regulations, the booklet includes several pages of material on basic school supplies and toiletry items which the student will need, and outlines the exact type of attire appropriate to various campus activities and events. It even includes reminders about such things as "coat hangers, [a] radio or record player, [a] shoe shine kit, and [a] tin box for food" which will make their dormitory room "more homelike." The lists obviously contain subtle hints about good grooming as well as expressing an attitude of parental concern for the student's comfort.

Central State also recognized that a higher proportion of its students entered with cultural as well as social disadvantages. The president's report for 1956 noted: "We know from testing Freshmen that our students come to us without adequate mastery of the tools of culture that are all but indispensable for the mastery of genuine college instruction." To the end of rectifying these disadvantages, improvements were mandated in both instruction and evaluation during the 1951–1965 years. Concurrently, the institution strove to maintain "quality" in its own cultural atmosphere. In the words of Dr. Wesley:

54

We shall be neither highbrow or lowbrow but . . . we shall become a college of quality at its best in individual and collective activity and in the practice of the highest and best standards of our culture. It means that our music must not be exclusively that of Basin Street, Beale Street, Lenox Avenue, 47th Street, or U Street. It must be also the music of the Masters which we will patronize. Our manners must not be those of Shanty-town and the Fish-house. They must be manners of ladies and gentlemen in all relationships. It means that our conduct and conversation must not be typical of the streets and the common place, for we are supposed to rise above these.

And it must be remembered that the same President Wesley who here argues so eloquently for cultural mainstreaming also introduced the college's first African studies program and supported the establishment of an African museum at the school. It was this fine harmony of particular ethnic and broader cultural objectives that led Wesley to conclude:

One of our great needs at this college has been that of inner direction rather than direction from the outside, or the imitation of that which goes on in other colleges and institutions. [13]

And it was that sense of inner direction which set it apart from other northern, rural, and predominantly black schools.

While the growth of Central State depended upon its ability to recognize and provide for the unique needs of a largely black student body, it was equally necessary for it to remain officially "colorblind" during this period of nationwide racial and academic turmoil. Wesley told a meeting of the Cleveland City Forum in April 1956, "The North cannot point the finger of derision at the South. Prejudice is not sectional." Neither was it peculiar to one race. To guard against possible charges of reverse discrimination and to implement its goal of integration, Central State kept no record of the racial composition of its student body during these years. Moreover, it refused to repose in the evidence of its superiority over other "black schools"; it insisted upon competing with all other colleges in its pursuit of academic excellence.

One example of this competitive spirit surfaced in 1956 in response to the army's nationwide testing of ROTC graduates. Several colleges in the deep South had a deplorable failure rate—in some cases as high as 75 percent. Central State then might well have pointed with pride at its own 34 percent rate of failure—the lowest of all United States colleges with a predominantly black enrollment. Wesley focused instead on the fact that the national average of army officers failing, excluding the black officers,

55

was only 14 percent. Wesley said, "This is a rather serious deficiency. . . . We are competing with standard colleges in our area and we shall certainly not be justified in being satisfied with any less than ranking well with our sister institutions in Ohio."[14]

Nor was success among its graduates the only area in which Central State strove to excel during these years. Although in 1951, faculty members holding doctoral degree numbered only fourteen, only a decade later this number had risen to thirty of the seventy-one faculty, or 42.2 percent. This figure placed the school well above average according to an evaluation by the North Central Association of Colleges and Secondary Schools. The association also ranked Central State's faculty above average in percentage of persons holding the master's degree.

In that same year, 1960–61, the administration found that they were keeping pace with or surpassing other schools in their renovation of the teacher training program at Central State. In August 1960, the New York State Board of Regents had voted to double approximately the minimum standards for teachers of academic subjects. The new requirements, however, had little effect on the course of study at Central State because they had already upgraded their program to similar levels.

As final evidence of the pursuit of excellence which enhanced Central State's development during this period is its early establishment and maintenance of the honors program for exceptional students. It is interesting that in 1960 Wesley expressed his concern that the faculty "give special attention to the gifted and the talented providing them with advice and additional guidance rather than to devote major attention to marginal students."[15] Far from indicating an elitist atmosphere at Central State, this reflects the school's philosophy that the recognition of special achievement will motivate all students.

Although factors thus far discussed have pointed to administrative attitudes and policies as the cause of Central State's uniqueness in the North, the faculty and the students themselves had equivalent roles in shaping its character. The forcefulness of the faculty is most clearly evidenced in their response to the 1965 investigation of alleged fiscal irresponsibility and de facto segregation. Departing from the general practice of faculties to remain silent on such matters or to speak through official college channels, the Central State faculty issued a statement to the media deploring "the mishandling of public funds by any person at any time, whether that person is of the administration, faculty, staff or other official agency of this State." They also denounced claims that the college was racially "closed," citing the approximate number of non-Negro students and faculty and pointing out that the school "had taken positive steps to advertise its position that this is indeed an interracial, intercultural, and international institution."[16]

Students, too, have pointed with pride to Central State's open door to all racial groups. In a 1962 issue of *The Gold Torch,* for example, a student editor stated, "Established in 1951 with an almost exclusively Negro student body, Central State has seen the number of white students increase almost 20 percent in recent years."[17]

But perhaps the most dramatic demonstration of the spirit of the college, which set it apart from others both in the North and the South, is an incident which occurred in May 1961. Two white Central State College students made news when they were arrested in Jackson, Mississippi "for attempting to integrate a 'white only' bus station lunch room."[18] Their decision to serve jail sentences to emphasize their protest of the unfair practice underscores one of the important differences in the Central State social environment which augmented its rapid development.

A second distinctive feature which contributed to the development of Central State College during the late 1950s and early 1960s was its strongly religious moral atmosphere. Just as it assumed a quasi-parental role in improving its students socially, culturally, and academically, so it was willing to maintain tough moral and ethical standards. Several methods for maintaining these standards are evidenced in documents issued by the college. They include institutional structures, positive guidelines and examples, psychological influence, and, of course, disciplinary action.

The importance of religion to the college becomes immediately apparent in reading the president's report to the Board of Trustees for 1950–51, in which several sections are devoted to religious matters. In outlining the goals of the educational program, Wesley stresses the need to foster

> a fully integrated personality and not merely a mind crammed with sufficient facts to pass the required examinations and accumulate the total units of credit. We expect our graduates to have personal integrity, character, human understanding and stable conduct. . . . Here students of various religions . . . may live in mutual respect and complete fellowship.

And there was indeed a great variety of religious affiliation at Central State. No less than twenty-seven different denominations, including five Methodist sects, were listed by students for the student personnel files for the 1950–51 academic year. More importantly, of the 769 students only 11 responded that they had "No Affiliation." Also significant are the percentage distributions among the represented denominations. Five hundred eighty-one of the 769—or approximately 75 percent—belonged to denominations which might be termed "Fundamentalist Protestant," among these the African Methodist Episcopal church, responsible for the college's original founding.

The strength of the students' religious ties is further indicated by the breakdown of Ohio and non-Ohio residents in this same report. Four hundred thirty-eight students came to Central State from outside Ohio—in spite of the fact that these out-of-state students were required to pay one and one-half times more for tuition and registration fees than were Ohioans. While it may be that these out-of-state students were attracted to Central State because of its rural location or its racial makeup, combined with its academic reputation, there are strong indications that many young people were urged toward Central State through their religious affiliations, particularly those attending Baptist and African Methodist Episcopal churches. Clearly the expansion of Central State was stimulated by its reputation for moral uprightness and religious tolerance.

One of the primary forces behind this reputation was the school's institutional structure for encouraging religious fellowship. In addition to employing a director of religious activities and maintaining a religious emphasis program, several clubs and organizations were encouraged to establish on-campus branches. Among these were the YMCA and YWCA, the Canterbury Club for Episcopal students, the Newman Club for Catholics, the Roger Williams Club for Baptists, the Wesley Foundation for Methodists, and the Westminster Club for Presbyterians.

Positive rules and guidelines also played a role, as did the example set by the behavior of faculty and administration. In 1951, for example, the college instituted a procedure both for students on probation and for those nearing probationary status. It specified that a "check, with comments by the teachers indicating what they think is the cause of the deficiency and what ought to be done, will be made at six-week intervals and cleared through the Office of the Dean of Academic Administration." Although this rule relates to academic problems, the system of faculty and administrative support and control extended beyond the classroom. If a student's extracurricular activities were interfering with studies or attentiveness in class, here was an official channel through which to inform and counsel the student toward improvement. For prospective students and their parents, the attraction of this system over a simple probation and dismissal procedure is apparent—particularly if the students' profiles predisposed them to academic difficulties.

58

Another quite different example of the establishment of positive guidelines may be found in the 1957–58 "Guide Book For Freshmen and New Students." This booklet, mailed to prospective students, devotes two full pages to the topic "Learn to Live with a 'Roomie.'" This section instructs the young person that "getting along with a roommate is helpful education for the give and take of a later career," and warns "Mind your manners, your tongue and your temper." This, too, indicates the extent of the school's involvement in the student's personal life and shows the moral tone set for the campus during the expansion years.

In addition to presenting the students with written guidelines for shaping or altering their behavior, President Wesley expected his fellow administrators and his faculty to influence the students as role models. In a 1960 address to the faculty, he designated two areas in which he thought such examples important. One of these was studiousness. "It is not too often," he admonished, "that I see faculty members using the library." He acknowledged that "some of us know what is there and accordingly need not make use of it," but added that "it would be well [for faculty] to set the example for students who are jointly in the pursuit of knowledge."

In this same address he spoke with even greater emphasis, however, of the need for faculty and administrators to provide moral and spiritual models of behavior:

> We hope that some of us will get out of bed on Sabbath mornings, set the example and attend the worship services. I am aware that this advice will fall immediately on deaf ears and that there may actually be some resentment and yet I make it in the interest of our expression of religion as a way of life and as a factor in campus quality. We should seek to show our belief that mankind is surrounded by, inspired by and challenged by spiritual impulses and that those who contact these impulses may be guided in worthy paths of life. Our campus atmosphere would be expanded through a common approach to a reverent, spiritual experience in words and music based upon the varying backgrounds of our students.[19]

This is an extraordinarily strong statement of religious philosophy to be encountered in the official documents of a secular college, and indicates the extent to which Central State stood apart from other state institutions in this regard.

While guidelines and examples might encourage morality among the student body, more substantial methods were also at work during Central State's expansion years. Discipline from within was the ultimate goal, but the school took steps to limit the students' occasions for backsliding. Both moral and academic improvement were intended in a 1960–61 rule to control campus social events. This rule provided that social affairs, including meetings of clubs "which ultimately are social gatherings," should be held only on Fridays and Saturdays, while Monday through Thursday "should be nights devoted to study and intellectual pursuits." Wesley reminded the faculty that in instituting this policy "we should not have hesitation in limiting the opportunities [young people] seek for social display and entertainment"—surely an attitude attractive to the parent or clergymen steering a high school student toward a college choice.

Wesley believed that student behavior on campus was subject to a sort of domino effect, and that when "The prevailing culture provides that a student should not study too much in class or take his college work too seriously or make noises in the dormitory, the culture has a way of bringing [a] student under control." Thus he advocated the use of psychological forces by the faculty to promote a reversal of this trend and to block the threat of peer domination or rejection from shaping students' behavior.

Ultimately, however, Central State, like most other colleges in this era, had to resort to sterner measures to maintain the moral climate on which the school had been built. In November 1965, the Committee on Student Services established guidelines for "offenses requiring student dismissals." In addition to the expected restraints on plagiarism, possession or sale of narcotics, drugs, or weapons, and destruction of school property, the committee also judged the following acts deserving of dismissal:

> Gambling and games of chance, . . . hazing, terrorism, vandalism, or acts that will tend to frighten, degrade, injure, disfigure, or that will cause physical or mental anguish, . . . possessing liquor [or] disorderly conduct while under the influence of alcoholic beverages, . . . absence from the dormitory without leave, male students involved with female . . . , [and] behavior involving moral turpitude.[20]

The inclusion of so many offenses of a purely moral and ethical nature is reflective of the continued religious emphasis at Central State. Moreover, the guidelines provided that "when cases are clear-cut, the Personnel Department can react with only the chairman's approval." The responsibility for adjudication and enforcement of campus behavior was clearly in the hands of the administration.

While the high ethical and spiritual standards of an institution may easily be seen to appeal to parents or other adults who might be counseling students on their college choice, might it not prove threatening or stifling to the students themselves? In the case of Central State in the mid-1960s, the answer was apparently, no. In the same year that the previously mentioned guidelines were established, the staff of the student newspaper spoke out plainly and unreservedly against some of the less wholesome trends in American student life. Addressing the new students in their traditional "welcome" editorial they stated: "We are now a University that demands new habits of study, research and individual responsibility. . . . We are not and will not be a haven or hide-away for 'Jitterbugs,' addicts or felons; these must quickly be identified and eliminated without favor or fanfare."[21]

The college had grown because of the strong religious influence and the tough moral and ethical standards of its whole operation—concern for individual students and pressure on all students for clean, wholesome living and responsible actions. It is significant that these student writers equated their pride in Central State's newly acquired university status with the need to uphold and even improve its moral character.

Many of the factors affecting the growth of Central State can be assessed in material, or at least perceptible terms, but perhaps the greatest shaper of the institution's character during the expansion years was the character of the man at its helm. Charles Wesley influenced Central State's development both from without—by virtue of the respect his scholarly reputation brought to the school—and from within—by virtue of his winning personality, his farsightedness, and the strength of his leadership.

Just how great an asset a highly visible and esteemed college president is to an institution—whether in terms of exceptional students enrolled, eminent faculty attracted, grants won, or the like—is impossible to determine. However, it is certain that Wesley's publications between 1951 and 1965 remained prodigious and his personal recognitions and honors increased. An issue of *The Gold Torch* from March 1965 lists the following publications by Wesley during his years at Central State: *The Little Sphinx: A History of the Improved Benevolent and Protective Order of Elks of the World* (1955), *The History of the Prince Hall Grand Lodge of Free and Accepted Masons of the State of Ohio* (1961), *Ohio Negro in the Civil War* (1962), *Negro Makers of History* (1958), *The Story of the Negro Retold* (1959), and *Negro in Our History* (1962). The latter three publications were co-authored by Dr. Carter G. Woodson. Numerous articles from scholarly periodicals are also cited. Wesley once remarked that he believed "a teacher who is without successful experience as a productive scholar is not fulfilling the complete purpose of his college appointment."[22] And he followed this tenet not only as a teacher but throughout his career as an administrator.

The Gold Torch also lists Wesley's organizational awards, including: The Diamond Jubilee Citation of the Kentucky Educational Association (1951), The Certificate of Award and placement on the Honor Roll of the John Brown Gallery of Fame of the Improved, Benevolent, Protective Order of the Elks of the World (1955), the 50th Anniversary Founders Award of the Alpha Phi Alpha Fraternity (1958), and the Gold Medal Award of the United Supreme Council of Scottish Rite Masonry, 33rd Degree, Prince Hall Affiliation, Southern Jurisdiction (1958).

A further indication of his scholarly acclamation lies in the elected offices that he held during his tenure at Central State. In 1954 and 1955, he served as president of the Association of College Presidents and Deans for the Ohio College Association. In 1956, he presided over the Midwest Conference on Discrimination and became a member of the board of directors of the Great Lakes Mutual Life Insurance Company based in Detroit, Michigan. This latter position is significant in two respects. First, it indicates that Wesley was known in the business as well as the academic world. And second, since he was the first director elected from outside Michigan, it shows the breadth of his reputation. He also served for more than ten years in the national post of secretary-general of the Scottish Rite Masons. In 1952 he was elected president of the Association for the Study of Negro Life and History in Washington, D.C. His service to this organization was so significant that the Charles H. Wesley Research Fund, to provide money for research in Negro history, was established in his honor. Central State faculty, staff, alumni, and students participated in a campaign to raise $50,000 for this fund in 1965. Upon his retirement from Central State in that same year, he became the association's director of research. Finally, Wesley was the first Negro to become president of the Ohio Colleges and Allied Societies. He did so in 1963, breaking the organization's ninety-two-year color barrier, and that of all similar associations in other states.

In examining these many achievements, one can see that Wesley knew and made use of his exceptional talent for getting along with and influencing people. He viewed his public relations responsibilities not as a respite from campus life, but as a vital, integral part of being a college president.

Valuable as Wesley's scholarly status and off-campus contacts may have been to Central State, what mattered most were the personal qualities and skills he applied to the day-to-day operation of the school. One of the most important of these traits—particularly appealing to students—was his humility. Upon his retirement in 1965, many encomiums appeared in *The Gold Torch* and elsewhere. One student dedicated the words, "If you can walk with kings . . . nor lose the common touch, yours is the Earth and everything in it." She went on to recall that Wesley did indeed feel equally at home with many different sorts of people. He had, for example, once talked with President John F. Kennedy, yet he "always found the time for persons who needed his help."[23] Just how did he make students feel so welcome and comfortable? Another student, the co-editor of *The Gold Torch,* related this incident in his letter of tribute:

> All of the guests, faculty and students [at a dinner sponsored by sociatas literatai] were standing about chatting when he arrived. There were the usual hello's and friendly exchanges. Being one of several inconspicuous freshmen who were all crowded in one corner, I felt my stomach jump into my throat when Dr. Wesley came our way. I guess he started introducing himself to each individual as he came toward me. By the time he had reached me, I had thought of a thousand things to say, but none seemed appropriate.
> "Hello. I'm Dr. Wesley."
> "How do you do?" I replied meekly. "I'm Quentin Burgess, from Plainfield, New Jersey."
> "Oh yes, your high school is very highly recommended; it is one of the best. Good luck here at Central, Mr. Burgess."
> He had moved on to the next bewildered individual. In that brief conversation, I felt that I was somebody, not just a pawn in a college community.[24]

Judging from the number and the sentiment of the many such tributes published in the months just prior to Wesley's departure, incidents like Burgess's must have occurred quite commonly.

Similarly, Wesley himself attributed his success in dealing with students simply to knowing and liking them. "We must have," he told his faculty in 1960, "a high sense of humor and not be a sourpuss in and out of the classroom or office; we must have the qualities of good will and kindness."[25] For Wesley, the students of Central State College were both a responsibility and a pleasure. This attitude filtered down through all levels of campus life and undoubtedly contributed to the school's growth.

Probably one of the sources of Wesley's good will to all was his deep religious devotion. Wilbur Allen Page, a former member of the college's board of trustees, spoke of this in his tribute to Wesley: "In addition to his great strength of character and religious convictions, with great humbleness of heart, he came, [and] gave to us his last full measure of devotion, . . . he proved to be a man whose heart God had touched." Indeed, one might say that Wesley showed an almost religious devotion to the school itself, accepting the position in 1942 for "a meager salary in comparison to the high standard of Howard University,"[26] weathering many storms of controversy, and remaining to the age of seventy-three—long past the age at which many of his counterparts had retired to more relaxing pursuits.

Wesley's religious beliefs may also have formed the basis of his strength of conviction, making him a man unafraid to meet the challenge of difficult tasks or of adversity. In 1963, for example, Wesley pledged his efforts and encouraged the alumni, students, and friends of Central State to do likewise. The occasion was the November general election in which Ohio voters were asked to approve a $25,000,000 bond issue for education. He reminded his audience that "one often gets out of a working project as much as he puts into it," and urged that they "put [their] best efforts forward; redoubling [their] efforts between now and the election; writing home to parents, to friends, and to alumni, asking them to vote for this issue."[27] He sought to convince them that his own method of facing such challenges as "an individual and personal effort" could bring success. He also suggested they campaign for local bond issues for building in nearby Xenia and surrounding Greene County. "As the local school system advances, we too advance." This was the philosophy around which Wesley attempted to shape Central State College: dedicate yourself to a worthy goal, labor to complete it, and share the fruits of that labor unselfishly.

Nowhere is this philosophy more apparent than in his firm, plain-spoken, and lifelong advocacy of racial equality and integration. Certainly his scholarly writings remained focused on these subjects throughout his career, but two more dramatic incidents better illustrate the impact of Wesley's principles on Central State. The first of these occurred in 1957, some years before civil rights had become a fashionable liberal cause. On April 1, just a few weeks before the end of the school year, Central State admitted three transfer students from Alcorn A & M College in Alcorn, Mississippi. These students had been expelled for participation in a student strike protesting the ethics of a history professor who had written "degrading articles against the NAACP in a local white Metropolitan paper." Wesley issued the statement that Central State would "readily accept these three students and would exhaust every legal means possible to attain their transcripts if they were not turned over."[28]

Wesley took an even more courageous stand in May 1957 on an issue much closer to home. He refused to allow any Central State College student to participate in the town of Xenia's Memorial Day parade, citing as his reason that small community's segregation practices. Coming at a time when Kent State University's administration was being criticized for its failure to rectify a campus housing bias, this brought Wesley and Central State even more into the state's civil rights spotlight.

Clearly, Wesley's strong moral and political stand on racial issues was a major asset in the school's development. Not only was such a supportive racial environment attractive to black students and faculty, but the media coverage drawn by Wesley's bold actions kept subtler forms of bias in check. He made it no secret that he thought Ohio's state legislature was not entirely innocent of such subtle biases, and on this quieter front as well he battled.

Despite Wesley's courage and energy, he never let the ideals he imagined for Central State's future obscure the practical issues of its present. He was neither a dreamer nor a promoter of panaceas, and he was not afraid to throw the harsh light of reality on others' flights of fancy. In the 1963 campaign for the state bond issue previously mentioned, he cautioned his audience that they should not view its passage as "the full answer to the problems of higher education in Ohio." In the same manner, he commented on his ambitious 1961–1963 capital improvements plan by noting, "We aren't interested in thinking about university status just yet. Our goal right now is to be the best college in the State."[29] Plans to seek university status were, of course, already in the works, and the building project was one of the cornerstones of those plans, but Wesley saw the wisdom in moderating the students' unreasonable hopes for a quick and easy approval. His blend of idealism tempered with good old-fashioned common sense was just what Central State needed during these years of rapid growth and change.

Wesley's humility, his humor, his morality, and his pragmatism all benefited the school over which he presided, but perhaps the quality of his personality which was most significant was his farsightedness. In his own words: "Surrounded by changes (in the economic and social life of our nation), in our knowledge, [and by] the development of new points of view, education cannot stand still." He saw to it that education at Central State did not. Yet he did not advocate change for the sake of change.

Three examples from his speech to the Faculty Institute in September 1960 serve to illustrate his compromise between traditional thinking and innovation. First, in projecting possible enrollment increases through the year 1967, he stressed that conservative estimates should be chosen. Second, in analyzing which course Central State should choose on the acquisition of new and very popular teaching machines and electronic testing devices, Wesley said, "Our opinion, however, is that no mechanical gadgets, no workbooks, films, tests or study machines can take the place of a superior teacher in association with students. Teaching equipment is one of our next important budget steps. We have made this program secondary to salary." And finally, regarding the nature of the curriculum, he recommended a movement away from strictly information-based study. "A college program of quality will be more than the traditional presentation of text material in a routine manner. Such a program will give opportunity for students to work with ideas and develop their relations to spiritual, moral and social problems."[30] In charting a course for Central State through the rapidly changing educational environment of the early 1960s, Wesley correctly judged that the trend toward more affective and cognitive-based curricula would be more beneficial to Central State than the one toward programmed and mechanized instructional materials, and he allocated the school's scarce funds accordingly.

Wesley's method of implementing this sort of far-sighted planning was to charge his planning committees with three types of tasks: (1) to seek out answers to specific, pressing questions by asking faculty and staff to assess these questions in their areas, (2) to formulate a short-term plan, typically two to five years, based upon this data, and (3) to offer more speculative suggestions for the long range, say ten to fifteen years in the future. Two of the most vital building and development phases in Central State's expansion period were planned in this manner.

In 1954, for example, the Faculty Committee on Planning was directed to "plan for the years 1954 to 1965 in one period of normal development and from 1965 to 1970 in the other as a period of upsurge in college enrollment." They were also, however, given the more immediate objective of obtaining and collating responses to four key issues: (1) the probable impact of impending nationwide educational integration, (2) the choice of breadth of program offerings versus specialization in two or three special areas, (3) the retrenchment, closure, or expansion of faculty, and (4) the most pressing needs for buildings or other physical facilities. Similarly, in 1961, a detailed capital improvements plan for the 1961–1963 biennium was coupled with a longer-range prospectus for seeking university status. Thus, Wesley always went to the board of trustees with both detailed and general proposals, and his careful planning paid off in allocations received.

Two specialized areas in which Wesley's farsightedness proved especially important relate to the racial makeup of Central State. As early as December 19, 1955, Wesley stated in an interview for the *Dayton Daily*

News, "Banning segregation is a two-way proposition. . . . Not only must Negroes be permitted to attend schools formerly restricted to whites according to the recent Supreme Court Decision, but we must make ourselves good enough to attract white students." He stressed that nothing in the curriculum was addressed exclusively to a Negro clientele and also noted that the school was making conscious efforts to attract white students, faculty, and even members of the board of governors.

At the same time, however, Wesley did not ignore any advantage that Central State might hold because of its tradition of an almost exclusively black student body. In 1961, he was instrumental in establishing the Department of American Affairs, a special unit to train blacks for diplomatic service and positions of leadership in Africa. He stated his belief that, by virtue of not only its attractiveness to highly qualified black students, but also its large enrollment of foreign students, Central State had "more of a foundation for such a program than any other state college or private college." Thus, this unit and other specialized programs related to African or black American culture were brought to Central State.

Charles H. Wesley is clearly an administrator of many talents who brought to Central State College the combined benefit of his skillful direction and his scholarly acclaim. Wilbur Allen Page best summed up Wesley's contribution in this way, "He is a leader who is never satisfied. He believes when one becomes satisfied, he stops growing."[31] Indeed, under his watchful direction, from 1951 to 1965, Central State never stopped growing.

four

The Era
of Instability

As might be expected after a tenure of more than two decades by such a forceful president, Central State's search for a replacement was not an easy one. Dr. Lewis A. Jackson, a faculty member at the school since 1946, was tapped to step in as acting president while a permanent replacement was sought. He had been promoted first to dean of the college and later to vice-president during Wesley's administration and, in his own words "accepted his [Wesley's] philosophy and direction. . . . In our planning sessions, he often expressed principles in which I concurred."[1]

Jackson was not, however, merely a carbon copy of his mentor. Serving in such a tenuous capacity and for less than one academic year, he nevertheless "made decisions as if [I] were to be president continuously." At the same time, he recognized that his time in office allowed faculty and administrators to feel "considerable freedom" in their attempt to obtain a more permanent administrator. His policies and actions kept Central on an even keel, and although they did not immediately result in his being offered the presidency, they afforded him that position later.

The "permanent" chief administrator whom the board of trustees appointed on December 1, 1965, was a man quite unlike his predecessor. A much younger man than Wesley, and cut from a different academic and generational mold, Dr. Harry E. Groves moved rapidly to establish a "modern collegial form of university governance."[2] Quite apart from Jackson, he had never met his predecessor, but clearly saw not only the positive but also the negative aspects of Wesley's reign. Groves had said of Wesley, "It was clear that he had administered the school in the old fashioned way of the black president as the all-powerful sole decision maker. He was also, apparently, a warm father-figure who treated faculty and students as parts of an extended family of which he was the unquestioned head." This was clearly not a model to which Groves, as successor, aspired.

Groves's training as a lawyer strongly influenced his personal style of decision making, but more important to the faculty and his fellow administrators were his experiences as a dean at Texas Southern, where the president, "unlike many black presidents . . . , delegated real authority to deans." An even more significant influence had been his years at the University of Singapore—a school operated on the English university model. The system to which he had become accustomed, first as a department head and later as a dean, at the University of Singapore was one in which professors essentially governed themselves through a powerful senate. Given the nationwide pressures for greater academic freedom that marked the 1960s, selection of a man like Groves to take Central State's helm seemed logical. Those who wanted a new style of leadership were not disappointed. Groves set to work immediately on sweeping changes.

Two major innovations were the creation of a faculty senate and the delegation of genuine authority to deans and department heads. No longer were all personnel and salary decisions made by the president alone. Salary schedules were openly discussed, and for the first time department heads and deans were taught to prepare a budget—and made responsible for that budget once in place.

For years, campus political issues, and particularly personnel shortcomings, had been like overworn chairs concealed by decorous antimacassars. The faculty had grown accustomed to having the decisions that were made for them, however arbitrary, couched in charm. Now things would be different. Groves weighed no words, spared no feelings. Although he felt it inappropriate for a president to come in with a ready-made reorganization plan and informed the assembled faculty that he "would not have done so if you had a plan that made any sense at all,"[3] he refused to operate for even a few months under the old comfortable system.

In retrospect, it is not difficult to see why he was so adamant about immediate reparation. Wesley—himself such an honorable and productive administrator—had clearly trusted too unquestioningly that all his subordinates were equally dedicated. Groves reported some of his more shocking discoveries to the Board of Trustees:

DR. HARRY E. GROVES
PRESIDENT (1965)

Scarcely any of [the University's] periodic reports required of all state schools by the Board of Regents and by the federal educational agencies in Washington were submitted on time. It was simply routine for these agencies repeatedly to have to request and demand late reports from this university. It had even failed to bill the Peace Corps for a training project that it had conducted more than a year earlier and for which the Corps owed the University more than $211,694.00 which the Corps was eager to pay in order to be able to close its books on the transaction. One of my first acts was to discharge the official directly responsible for this fiasco. When we checked his filing cabinet we found more than $10,000 in cash and in uncashed checks received by the University as much as three years earlier. Even checks from the State of Ohio were found simply stuffed in folders in filing drawers.[4]

No longer would across the board pay raises go "to the competent and incompetent alike." He chided the faculty also for their noninvolvement with fund raising or with writing grants to bring in development dollars. About their general lack of scholarly publication he was scathing:

I was appalled when I learned that the library here has been accustomed to closing during the Christmas vacation. I have been working at schools where the president would have been tarred and feathered by the faculty if he had permitted the library to be closed for such a period. I am told that you people could not care less and that if you show up in any numbers in the library it will be regarded as a prelude to the second coming.

He went on to lament the fact that "the rigors of tenure make it difficult to remove academic deadwood," but warned administrators, who lacked that protection, to "stand aside now" and make it "less painful for us all" to effect changes.[5]

Business matters were also reorganized. Fiscal policy was updated. With university monies no longer held in non-interest-bearing checking accounts, the school netted thousands of dollars in interest each year.

Groves was as blunt in the assessment of the university's financial problems, which he made to the Alumni Association less than five months after his arrival, as he had been with the faculty:

No American state-supported university in this period can hope to reach its fullest potential solely on the support the State provides. I was appalled to find that Central State had made so little attempt to develop by seeking federal government resources or by approaching the great Foundations with worthwhile development projects. We are trying to rectify this neglect of the past, moving very rapidly in our attempts to catch up.

By August 1966, he could point with pride at some significant gains in federal grants. For the 1965–66 academic year, Central State received $675,000 for buildings, $37,800 for electronic equipment, $35,000 for summer institutes, $123,823 for the promising new Upward Bound Program, and over $800,000 for student loans and other direct student financial aid.[6]

The Upward Bound Project is indeed one of the most outstanding reminders today of Groves's short stay at Central State. Headed at its inception by Drs. John C. Alston and Ames W. Chapman, it brought in non-college-bound high school sophomores and juniors for an eight-week respite of counseling, education, and cultural enrichment. Even the children's medical, dental, and optical needs were met during the summer, and monthly returns to campus during the academic year were written in to provide meaningful follow-up.[7] The program has also proved to be a successful recruitment tool in succeeding years.

Other changes, though not as dramatic as those in fiscal and academic policy, produced admirable gains in efficiency and responsiveness. One example of this was the introduction of more orderly procedures in the office of the registrar, reducing the frustration and delay for those requesting transcripts. When this registrar retired in 1967, letters from graduates were found dating back to 1964 requesting transcripts. Not only had the requests lain unanswered, but the checks that had accompanied them were left undeposited.

Increased responsiveness was also the goal of redefining some faculty and administrative roles. Again, just seven days after assuming his place as president, Groves announced that henceforth only "teachers and librarians" would be termed faculty. This prefaced his decision that all administrative offices should remain open during school holidays. "I think it is because of your incorrect concept of the roles of the faculty and the administration," he told the nonacademic staff, "that you have been accustomed to closing. . . . I can see why much of your work is behind with such poor practices."[8]

In even more forthright language than he had used on the faculty, he pointed out the shortcomings of the nonacademic staff and outlined his expectations for improvement. There was no place for any employee who was "rude and ill-tempered toward students or faculty," who deserve to be treated with at least the courtesy they would get as a "customer in a bank or department store." Written communications were no longer to be left "to gather dust in someone's file," but rather were to be answered "within twenty-four hours." Groves was also talking about the other mundane activities of campus life:

> . . . such things as registration, fee paying, getting meal tickets and the thousands of other matters involved in administration. I have seen institutions where students get the run around in administrative offices, where their problems are brushed off or ignored, where their time is considered to be worthless and they are required to make numerous trips to an office to accomplish what should have required no more than one trip. You may know of such an institution. If so, you know one where the administration concerned is inefficient.

If this "shoe" brought an uncomfortable pinch to anyone seated in this meeting, they must have realized that the new president was talking about their job becoming "surplus" and themselves "expendable."[9]

Many of Groves's changes were unequivocally positive ones, but in retrospect his rush to "depersonalize the office of the president" may have been too much too soon. In exchange for the greater authority that he had entrusted to them, he required that his faculty and administrators settle their own minor problems. The door to the president's office would no longer be open to "gossip and trivial matters." Some who had worked long under the Wesley administration must have felt alienated by the new system. Asked to look back upon the decisions he made regarding university governance, Groves admits that, although they were the actions of which he is "most proud," he might have been "in less of a hurry in phasing in many changes which were disliked. . . . I might have paid more attention to the psychology of change."

The pace of social change in the mid-1960s was indeed so rapid that the country as a whole, and university life in particular, could scarcely afford the luxury of inquiring more carefully into its "psychology." Students nationwide were vocal and often violent in their demands for personal, academic, and sexual freedom. The black power movement, with roots in both the broader civil rights crusade and the anti-war protests, was rapidly gaining momentum. On historically black campuses—Central State among them—black students became increasingly resentful of the presence of both white students and white faculty. Perhaps in this volatile environment it was fortunate that Groves did not share with Wesley or Jackson the desire to increase the percentage of nonblacks within the university or to enhance multi-cultural opportunities.

In the mid-1960s Central State's minority white population made up approximately one-third of the faculty and 20 percent of the student body.

73

Yet Groves called it "incomprehensible why a formerly, or pre-dominantly white institution is integrated in the public mind when one Negro appears on the scene, whereas the fact of integration is doubted when there are literally hundreds of white persons in a predominantly Negro institution."[10] Although he "supported and protected the rights of whites to be there, the black power movement not withstanding," steps actively to encourage minority white enrollment and hiring were ended.

Like the students he governed, Groves's primary focus was in making Central State a bulwark of black culture and achievement. One increasingly thorny obstacle was the national profile of student bodies. From the time desegregation had become the rule rather than the exception in higher education, a major challenge to black colleges and universities had been the competition to attract highly qualified black students. Central State had long accepted, as part of its mission, the responsibility for raising many poorly prepared students to college level work. Far from considering this a burden, Groves acknowledged it as a unique and welcome challenge. "Predominantly Negro institutions, while freeing themselves of racial prejudice and racial limitations, can serve the greater cause of social uplift of the poor and educationally deprived, white and black, perhaps better than can other institutions," he said.[11]

However, during the 1960s and 1970s, the school walked yet another tightrope. How could they continue to foster students' pride in black history and heritage, yet avoid attracting a disproportionate number of black activists? Might more conservative parents shy away from sending their children to a campus known for its radical racial climate?

How many students and what kind of students should Central try to attract? Groves indicated in his inaugural address, delivered on October 20, 1966, that although he was concerned about "an environment of youth engaged in a restless search for place and purpose and identity," he and the university could handle this challenge as well. He viewed as advantages "the opportunities inherent in small size," and felt that Central State should "evaluate the qualities of smallness and plan for the preservation of those that are meritorious."[12] Yet like many short-sighted demographers of the time, he mistakenly assumed that America's upward population and economic curve would continue unabated—that "an expanding economy and an increase in social and economic expectations would be sending a vastly greater percentage" of the traditional 18- to 21-year-old group to college, and that Central must grow larger as rapidly as possible.[13] Whatever the cause, Central State's enrollment had climbed to over 2,200 by 1966.

Yet if students who heard of the new president's consideration of them as "customers" whom the university existed to serve believed that he would be soft on academic standards, they could not have been more wrong. He told them:

> I see today's student as a person who had better be in a hurry, who needs to be rushing towards excellence. It may be back in those gently halcyon days before World War I, when people fortunate enough to get to a university were so small in numbers and already so highly selected on the basis of family status and economic security, that four years in a university could be regarded as a time to play and to grow up. If this was ever so, it is not so now. Hundreds of thousands of students are in universities, . . . and in a competitive society the best reach the top, the good survive, the rest fall by the wayside. . . . I believe the future of every student is likely to be determined by the quality of the work he does here. I believe any student who sets for himself a lower standard than excellence has made the decision to cheat his future for all time, a manifestly stupid decision and one that is almost certain to be irretrievable.[14]

In the areas of speaking and writing especially, he chided them that their teachers had, in his opinion, been too lenient in their demands, and, that they themselves had been too content to fulfill these lowered standards. Nor was he reticent to point out his distress at the high "delinquency rate, crime rate [and] venereal disease rate" among members of their generation. But he told the students, too, that his primary reason for accepting the post at Central State was that he liked "working with young people, and this position [though it paid less than his current income] provides the greatest scope for that work."[15]

One aspect of campus life that changed only for the better during Groves's administration was Central State's contribution to the development of the black arts. In a convocation address delivered on November 1, 1966, at the approximate mid-point of his presidency, Groves outlined what he perceived to be the three most important roles of "predominantly Negro institutions of higher education." One of these roles was that:

> they must be the showplaces for the abilities and the talents, the history and the culture of the Negro people. . . . Until other institutions recognize and accept their own responsibilities in the premises, the predominantly Negro institutions must be the preservators of and instructors in the cultural and educational contributions of the Negro to America. In them the Negro's place in history must be taught. His contributions to literature must be preserved. His rich musical talents must find expression.[16]

75

To that end, Groves gave strong support to the music school, where, for example, he encouraged the performance of traditional spirituals. As a patron of the art department, he purchased several student works for his personal collection. Further, he encouraged the spending of money to bring noted black lecturers and performers to campus, always attending their presentations and inviting each of them to his home. Of greatest significance was his initiation of the effort to build a performing arts facility—an effort that was not to come to fruition until several years later.

On the whole, Groves was a well-organized administrator who sought to shape Central State through policies rather than politics, through colloquia rather than charisma. He encouraged and expected the same mature approach to responsibility from the faculty, the staff, and the students whom he governed. "In the final analysis, any 'impact' one has had [on students] may not be manifested for years," he said. Unfortunately, Harry Groves could not wait for those passing years to reward his efforts. For one thing, his deep love of the law and his understanding of the dangers of racial chauvinism set him sharply at odds with the student activists he was attempting to govern. Groves had personally witnessed the bloody racial conflict between the Malays and the Chinese during his last years in Singapore. He knew, too, that the "free universities [in California and elsewhere] where the entire operation is unstructured and totally democratic," were, "of course also unaccredited."[17] Surely no thinking student wanted this for Central State. He became increasingly perplexed and perturbed when the weight of his greater maturity and faultless logic failed to restrain campus demonstrations.

It may have been that Groves's logical and well-meaning initiatives toward more democratic decision-making powers were misperceived by students as concessions—as signs of weakness—and actually incited them to make greater demands. Under his administration, students for the first time had achieved representation on the Academic Senate. The elected student government controlled an $18,000 budget yearly—an amount larger than that allotted to some department heads. The management of the student newspaper rested for the first time in the hands of student editors. A Commission on University Relations had been formed to advise the president on how to improve communications on matters of importance to students. All this Groves had done, but still the students demonstrated and openly displayed their disrespect.

Had all the unrest arisen from the student body, and had the faculty and administrators represented a solid esprit de corps, Groves might yet have chosen to remain. But he came increasingly to realize the "many members of the University family were very comfortable with the institution they had and deeply and bitterly resent change." In his letter of resignation, dated November 25, 1967, he reproached those who "unable to attack me in the significant areas of my work"—an increase of 22 percent in enrollment and of 200 percent in federal financial support—"have subjected me to constant petty attacks." He concluded that

> in this hour of genuine institutional crisis, brought about by elements determined to destroy the University, I find many students, parents, alumni and faculty members not discussing the improvements and developments of the University, nor even the really basic issues threatening the life of the institution, but calling upon me to defend an allegation that I changed the route of march for graduation ceremonies and such equally inane charges. I was prepared for the larger battles. I am disgusted by the trivia.[18]

In 1968 he left his post, and Central State was once again in the market for a new president.

While Groves's selection as president had likely resulted primarily from the good impression he had made and ties he had formed with board members and government officials, influential faculty members figured prominently in the school's next choice.[19] Dr. Herman R. Branson, a scientist whose work at Howard University had brought him national recognition as a program manager, was selected. Branson had himself excelled early in an academic area not frequently chosen by minority scholars. After graduating cum laude in physics from Virginia State College and receiving his Ph.D. from the University of Cincinnati, he began a distinguished career of teaching and research at Dillard University. His eleven years at Howard were marked by a steady growth in the stature of the physics department and a pronounced increase in the number of students choosing careers in science. These successes were undoubtedly among the chief factors that prompted Central to select Branson. But at the same time, it was this knack for leadership and political ease that made Central State an attractive steppingstone on the way to more nationally influential posts.

Quite different from Groves, who approached leadership with an apparent air of reluctance, Branson seemed to take campus politics in stride. In an early "political" move in the fall of 1969, he appropriated a very sizeable sum for "updating and revitalizing all areas of the General

DR. HERMAN R. BRANSON
PRESIDENT (1968)

Alumni Office," created the paid staff position of director of development
and alumni affairs, and appointed the popular Walter G. Sellers to the
new post. The Alumni Association was understandably eager to embrace
the "new 'Dr. Branson Era.'"[20]

During his short time in office, he sought to establish more firmly the financial and managerial improvements made by Groves. He presided over balanced budgets and "built up morale in good people."[21] While Groves had tried, often in vain, to explain the complexity of university issues as a method of garnering support, Branson sought instead to reduce issues to their simplest elements. In one of his first addresses as president, Branson stated:

> We know how to make a first rate school in America; it's primarily a question of money. With a sympathetic Board and money, you can bring in top-flight people from anywhere and build up a program. If a Negro college did have proper resources and could design a program for young people of ability whose backgrounds may be weak, I don't doubt we could build up first rate programs in many places.[22]

Perhaps such an unsophisticated philosophy would work. Perhaps money was the primary ingredient that would make Central State a national leader. Branson made bold predictions about the course he was charting.

When the 1970–71 school year began, the university's enrollment had reached over 2,500, up by nearly 14 percent in just four years. On that basis, Branson predicted it would double to 5,000 by 1975 and double again to 10,000 by 1980[23]—predications that turned out to be vast exaggerations. Plans for a new dormitory, for example, called for an eventual total of eight buildings, each to house 150 students—nearly half again the number them enrolled. However if Branson's projections were wide of the mark, the methods he recommended for boosting enrollment and for securing new funds were right on target.

He continued Groves's initiatives to bring more federal grant dollars. Thanks to the expertise of Dr. DeField T. Holmes, then chairman of the university's grant proposal committee, an additional $190,000 was made available for special services for disadvantaged students. Central State's grant—the fourth largest of only 117 awarded nationwide—provided for tutorial assistance, health care, career planning, personal and psychological counseling, and basic skills improvements for "high risk" students with inadequate secondary school preparation.[24]

Branson also exhibited prescience in analyzing the future need for non-government funding. While not attempting to minimize the federal and state government's obligation to continued development of higher education, he candidly stated that "private sentiments are more effective than official statements." Alumni's special needs and interests would be served, but clearly more would be expected of them as well. "Additional assistance," he told them, "must come from Alumni and friends of the University." Also, with some reluctance, Branson recommended that the board of trustees increase tuition costs by over 50 percent (from $363 to $540 per year for an Ohio resident) and room and board by 14 percent (to $960 per year).[25]

One important improvement that could be achieved as a result of expanded revenues from various sources was a much needed increase in the salary range of faculty members. Branson thus would have one necessary tool to attract the new talent necessary to help Central State achieve its special growth potential.

He envisoned at least two avenues—both of which would later be exploited more fully—in which Central was uniquely suited to excel. The first of these was urban studies, not only because students could empathize with urban problems and had experienced urban education, but "because so many of our graduates go back to live and teach in the inner city."[26] Second, he foresaw the importance of Central's leadership in forming academic and cultural ties with African nations. During the summer of 1970, for example, CSU basketball Coach Bill Lucas and five of his key players were invited by the NAIA and the U.S. State Department to make a six-week tour of west and central Africa, conducting sports clinics in eight different countries. A man of actions rather than words, he set about "making Central State strong and clean."

Among the tasks of Branson's presidency was to secure continued accreditation by the North Central Association—a status hard won during the Wesley years. This was, in itself, a project that required most of the administration's attention during his short presidency. He had to answer not only the concerns of the association, but also the more nebulous questions of inadequacy raised by students, parents, tax payers, and legislators. He prided himself on having instilled "greater confidence in C.S.U." and in making students feel "more involved." As a way of illustrating the high status he accorded the teacher's role, and to remain in touch with the day-to-day needs of students, Branson maintained a six-hour teaching load in addition to his administrative duties.

Improved academic programs and an increased effort to get students into graduate and professional schools were among Branson's top priorities. He was particularly disdainful of the then rapid proliferation of state technical schools: "What all of us must do is to bring black students back into four-year colleges where they can succeed. It is criminal for 75 to 80 percent of blacks entering higher education to enroll in two-year colleges." With this philosophy in mind, Branson strove diligently to strengthen and sharpen curricula and to keep students' attention focused on academics in an increasingly changeable and violent political environment.

In spite of Central State's efforts to stay in touch with the student viewpoint, it was becoming increasingly clear here, as it was across the United States, that there must be limits set and enforced regarding control of the higher education process. In "An Address to the Faculty of Central State University" entitled "The University Looks at Itself," delivered by Vice-President Oscar Woolfolk in September 1969, the need for control was couched in the most diplomatic terms. It was nevertheless quite plain:

> No University can maintain its integrity or serve as a productive enterprise if . . . any one of the segments of the University attempts to take over the governing of the University in an autocratic manner. . . . A general assumption is that the faculty knows more than the students and that there is a master-apprentice relationship between teachers and students. . . . The advocacy of certain causes by student groups as well as faculty groups is presenting a serious challenge to academic freedom and eventually may lead to the destruction of academic freedom.

At the same time, Woolfolk was tough on any teacher who might believe that his or her responsibility had been fulfilled if only "the opportunity for scholarship" had been created. He charged them with the duty to "dig very deep to find methods and techniques for reaching the large number of poorly prepared students who come to us without vision or motivation." He envisioned Central State as a leader in redefining the purpose of universities not only to instruct the qualified and to conduct research, but to provide the "public service" of uplifting the academically disadvantaged.[27]

To many insiders on the Central State campus, it was clear from the time of his arrival that Branson was a man on the move. He traveled a great deal and was deeply involved in the national position of black colleges and black college students. On May 20, 1970, he led a delegation of twelve presidents of predominantly black colleges and universities in a two-hour meeting with President Richard Nixon. The meeting, which was reported on all major wire services and national television networks, was a major influence in Nixon's position on Title III legislation. It also vaulted Branson ever more rapidly into the public eye.[28] Ultimately, however, it may have been unsolvable mysteries about Central State's financial resources that prompted Branson eagerly to accept the proffered presidency of Lincoln University in Pennsylvania. Thus, in 1970, Central State found itself returning to an "insider": Lewis Jackson was now to become president in his own right.

Jackson was unique among Central State's presidents because, unlike his predecessors, his study and research as well as his practical experience was in education. While at Central, he had visited Nigeria, for example, to negotiate a cooperative affiliation with an African university. He earlier had ample opportunity as an undergraduate at Marion College and as a classroom teacher at both the elementary and high school levels to examine the process of learning. His graduate degree studies at Miami University of Ohio and his Ph.D work at The Ohio State University left him well versed in the principles of higher education and gave him a more thorough acquaintance with the public higher education system of Ohio than his predecessors had enjoyed.

Like Groves and Branson, Jackson understood the need to be "cost conscious and efficiency oriented,"[29] but to a greater extent than they, he viewed budget decisions in the larger context of the state-supported higher education system. Invidious comparisons of the situation at Central State with those at other public universities in Ohio had, in fact, brought alumni president Nancy T. Bolden to state in her 1970 message: "I am convinced that if the Alumni Association does not act *now* in this crisis, C.S.U. will not survive." Like many concerned members of the Central "family," Bolden blamed the state legislators and governor. She urged Ohio alumni to rally at the polls for "a State Administration that will stop using C.S.U. to pay off its political debts to lower echelon politicians— particularly Negroes in this category—who place little or no value on C.S.U. as an academic institution of higher learning."[30] Jackson certainly concurred with the Alumni Association's meeting with the governor regarding greater consideration for Central, but a goal that Jackson set for his administration, and which he now reemphasizes as a challenge for the future, is "competing with other colleges using taxpayers' dollars and providing equivalent education for equivalent costs."

Quite a few administrative and faculty changes took place during the years between 1970 and 1972, ranging from the naming of a new vice-president of academic affairs, John C. Alston, who replaced E. Oscar Woolfolk, to reorganization of physical plant services. Walter Sellers was promoted to head the newly created Office of University Relations, and was responsible not only for development and alumni affairs, but for information, sports publicity, and the print shop. A third new administrative post—director of institutional research and planning, created through

DR. LEWIS A. JACKSON
JOINED FACULTY (1946)
DEAN OF THE COLLEGE (1957)
DIRECTOR OF GRADUATE STUDIES (1969)
PRESIDENT (1970)

a grant from the United States Office of Education—was filled with a "newcomer," Dr. Warren Webber, formerly chairman of the Department of Fine Arts at Cedarville College. These new offices and the men appointed to them reflect Jackson's continuation of administrative streamlining begun under Groves and Branson. They reflect, too, his openness in personnel decisions and his dedication to seeking fresh, workable pedagogical strategies. During this same time period, over thirty new faculty members were hired and eight existing ones promoted.

Because of Jackson's broad pedagogical knowledge and experience, his became a student-centered rather than a program-centered administration. He acknowledged that his predecessors had had "concern for the welfare of the University [and] quality education for all students," but in his own words he had often felt that "all schools spent too much time on programs and too little finding out the unique abilities and capacities of students. . . . Programs should enhance students' special abilities to . . . reach their potential." With this in mind, Jackson attempted to "relate expenditures in terms of stated university goals and objectives so as to gain the most for students for each expenditure."

Although students were to be valued as consumers and all citizens treated in an open, friendly way, Central State's policy under Jackson was to hold them "accountable for their educational responsibilities and goals." It was assumed that those who matriculated were seeking a quality educational experience. Once there, they were expected to give their best effort. High standards and "endeavors to meet [those high] published standards" are well remembered by Central students of the early 1970s.

One highlight of this presidency which seemed to bode well for the future of academic innovation at Central State occurred late in 1971. As one of six American college administrators chosen by the American Association of State Colleges and Universities, Jackson spent four weeks in Western India visiting some twenty institutions of higher learning. Several possibilities for enhancing Central State's curriculum and its position came to light as a result of this trip. Jackson listed nine of them in an interview with the *Alumni Journal:*

—A re-examination of the total curriculum with respect to international content.
—More involvement and concern with foreign aid programs.
—Furnishing a cogent rationale for inclusion of more significant programs encompassing Asian culture, past and present.
—Stimulation of vital and pertinent exchange of faculty and students.[31]
—Intercultural incursion of a large segment of the American population now served by the state colleges and universities.

—Preparation of teachers with an international dimension who will, in turn, encourage an intercultural sensitivity in their students.

—Imbuing faculties with the importance of on-going effort to bridge intercultural differences and to communicate effectively.

—Development of faculty resources who might qualify as consultants to fill overseas requests of a short-term nature.

—Study and comparative analysis of common problems affecting health and national well being to learn what contributions can best be made by higher education on a world basis.[32]

In short, Jackson felt that the university had an opportunity to distinguish itself by developing an expertise in international studies—an area of increasing interest to the United States' business and economic sectors. At the same time, the experiences of India, a poor country with a burgeoning and largely illiterate population, might prompt fresh, creative approaches to reaching America's academically disadvantaged.

High achievement and the applied methods necessary to high achievement had first captured Jackson's attention in an arena outside the typical classroom. As director of training for the Division of Aeronautics and the Army Primary Flying School at Tuskegee during World War II, he had gained many insights, and his responsibility for examining applicants for pilot certificates for the Federal Aviation Administration had further strengthened his commitment to the integrity of high standards. It was for this reason that Central State's loss of accreditation to operate a graduate school affected him so deeply.

Jackson explains:

> One accrediting examiner of the North Central Association informed me that many persons at CSU had stated that the University's purpose was to help the poorly qualified minorities to do developmental work not available in other colleges. He said that the Association had withheld the graduate program because of the inconsistency between that mission and graduate studies. When he asked what I thought, I told him that it was an unfortunate experience, because it labels the school in a sense and it leaves some students to wonder why CSU is the only state university without a graduate program. It does not present an image of achievement such as exists elsewhere and may indicate that certain kinds of people are less qualified for graduate studies.

The loss of the graduate school was a doubly bitter one: first, because Jackson had served as director of the Graduate School and "understood the problems related to its closing as well as the problems of reestablish-

85

ing it," and second, because it interfered with his brightest hope for "operating the University as one for all Ohio students and others but not as a place for predominantly one race."

Of all Central State's presidents, Jackson remains the most emphatic in pressing for racial integration. He views it as an issue of "creating the kind of climate which will attract students regardless of race, primarily because of better educational achievement possibilities."

His efforts in this direction began while he served as dean of the college under Wesley's administration. Jackson at that time requested and received permission to develop a Committee on College-Community Relations, the purpose of which was to identify the school as a general purpose institution. Through the committee, Jackson had sought to illustrate his belief that in education as in "so many fields performance not color is the important factor." As a result of the work of this committee—a committee composed of faculty members of both races—an ever larger proportion of white students began to enroll. Jackson recalls that in one subsequent summer session, white enrollment actually exceeded black enrollment. The graduate program to which he was dedicated "enhanced white enrollment also—nearly 50 percent of the students at times were white."

Student and faculty relationships within the graduate school were excellent and served as a model and an inspiration to campus-dwelling undergraduates. Understandably, during his own presidency, Jackson sought to build on the policies and attitudes he had fostered during his years as dean. His broad vision of Central State—not only as a strong institution in its own right but as a strong, equitable partner in Ohio's public education system—prompted him to press again and again for greater integration efforts.

Such efforts, he felt, should be made not just to attract a racially mixed undergraduate enrollment but to appoint a racially mixed board of trustees. He brought this matter to the attention of Governor John Gilligan when the governor's office issued a press release pointing to the unusually large number of minority trustees he had appointed throughout the state. Why, Jackson asked the governor, do most institutions in Ohio have only one or no trustee[s] of minority origin, while most are "congregated at CSU?" Through his struggle to increase the nonblack presence at Central State, then, Jackson clearly hoped to improve the racial balance throughout Ohio's public universities. Reactions to his efforts—both from within the system and from without—were varied, and he found himself without the mandate for change that he wanted. In 1971, he was contacted by

Sinclair Community College in nearby Dayton, where he was much admired for his efforts at Central State. For the fifth time in less than a decade, a new pilot would be sought to steer Central through uncertain waters toward its centennial year.

five

The Rebuilding Years

By the time Dr. Lionel Hodge Newsom became president of Central State University in the autumn of 1972, he had seen many of his personal goals realized, had been at the cutting edge of both military and civilian desegregation, and had saved one university—Johnson C. Smith—from financial and academic chaos. At age fifty-three he came to Central State with intention of saving another one. Although Central was far from being in the deplorable state in which he had found Smith, it was clear that firm, consistent leadership was needed.

Newsom was surely aware of many of the challenges, both internal and external, which awaited him. But the greatest problems were those that no one could have predicted or prepared for: a political climate that would turn away from rigorous affirmative action and student financial aid programs; a national economy that would slip into a recession from which Ohio, with its heavy industrial base, could not completely rebound; and an overcast sky that would randomly drop a funnel cloud and take away three-quarters of the university.

During the first months of Newsom's administration, however, subtler issues held sway. His three immediate predecessors had chosen a decentralized, faculty-centered model of university governance, but Newsom adhered to the more traditional system of the Wesley years. It must have seemed to him from the very beginning that some long-tenured faculty members had resisted the new policies, and he keenly felt the pressure of the board of trustees to hold him accountable for all aspects of university operations. Jackson, who remained at Central State for two years after stepping down from the head office, recalls that some faculty members sought to retain authority also, and the Handbook for Faculty then became "a point of difference." Jackson says, "It is difficult to draw the lines carefully between the authority of the president and that of the faculty since in many areas there may seem to be overlapping authority. This concern was presented to me as a problem more than I had experienced previously or since."[1]

Perhaps, though, Newsom's style was less a movement away from faculty-centered governance than away from policy-centered governance. Although their methods were unlike, Jackson and Newsom agreed that students must always be the top priority. Newsom declares that his greatest similarity to Wesley was that

> both of us were in dead earnestness about educating as many students as we could. Neither of us thought there were too many, we always thought there were too few. Both of us felt that too many had been shortchanged educationally— through no fault of their own and that the State and Federal governments owed them the opportunity. With this in mind I believe we both felt it was appropriate to have a deficit because the State and Federal governments never provide adequate funds to accomplish the mission.[2]

After only six months in office, Newsom could see that it would require all of his persuasive skills to move the university ahead. His predecessors had made some progress, but none had stayed long enough to see projects through to completion. Moreover, the tip of the political scale toward conservatism had already begun. In April 1973, addressing the annual Off-Campus CSU General Alumni Association Conference, he warned that "institutions of higher learning are recognizing that the merry-go-round has broken down." Governor John Gilligan's first estimate of a 3 percent funding increase was painfully inadequate for schools such as Central State, where a small student body and an aging physical plant hampered attempts at growth. He acknowledged that the later proposed 5 percent would "permit" us not to cut so deeply, but still would not give "the finances for needed development and improvements."

In his usual forthright way, he pinpointed the specific share that the alumni chapters should contribute, criticizing their previous levels of support. "We know," he said, "we must give sacrificially to support these things that state and federal appropriations will not support."[3] His goal was nothing less than $100,000—an amount nearly equal to the endowment of both Central State and Wilberforce combined. They gave the new

DR. LIONEL H. NEWSOM
PRESIDENT (1972)

president a standing ovation, but would they as readily give him their money?

If they did not respond as quickly or as generously as he hoped, it may have been because in 1973 he was still a stranger to most of them. Aside from loyal members of the Alpha Phi Alpha fraternity, who no doubt knew him as that organization's able general president from 1965 to 1968,[4] the majority of alumni, like the faculty and students, were not familiar with Newsom's many accomplishments. He did not generally seek the limelight. At Smith he eschewed an elaborate formal inauguration, saying, "My father always said don't put a five dollar hat on a five cent head, so don't honor a man before he's done anything."[5] But in reality, Newsom had already done plenty.

Graduated cum laude from Lincoln University in Missouri with a double major in history and sociology, he immediately sought a master's degree in sociology from the University of Michigan. Following his mentor, the eminent sociologist Walter C. Reckless, to Ohio State, he there began doctoral work in the sociological aspects of criminology and anthropology. He would later recall that "as a student at Michigan and Ohio State, I did not know a black person on the full-time faculty"[6]—a fact that would later strengthen his convictions about the need for black role models in the professions.

Newsom's own Ph.D., along with his plans to marry a young school teacher, Maxine Emerson, were interrupted by World War II. It was during the course of the war that the United Stated Army became integrated, and Newsom was among the first few black candidates at the Officers Training School. Lieutenant Newsom completed his service in the Near East, assisting in quelling riots in Calcutta, India. The fresh perspective on America which he gained while abroad curbed his bitterness about U.S. race relations.

His interrupted doctorate was complete not at the Ohio State University, but rather at Washington University in his home city of St. Louis, where he would become its first black Ph.D. graduate. Dr. Newsom, with degrees in both anthropology and sociology, began his teaching career at Lincoln University. He supervised community services for the St. Louis Housing Authority for one year, then moved on to Southern University in Baton Rouge, a post he maintained for thirteen years. It was at Southern that his special interests in both the gifted and the disadvantaged student flourished. In addition to his duties as head of the newly formed Department of Sociology and Pre-Social Work, Newsom was chairman of a Pre-School Conference on Identification of the Superior Student and the Development of His Special Attitudes. Yet at the same time he taught (as a volunteer) a twenty-eight-week Great Books course for state prison inmates.

In 1960, Newsom resigned, along with several other Southern University professors, in protest of the expulsion of students involved in the

Baton Rouge civil rights movement. No longer would Newsom's struggle for racial equity be merely a personal one. His next academic post at Morehouse College in Atlanta would deepen his involvement even further. He was a professor of sociology there in 1961, when the school instituted an honors program financed through the Woodrow Wilson Foundation. As the program's director and faculty adviser, he had an opportunity to test his belief that "undergraduates [sophomores in this case] grouped in this way stimulate one another and reach a more mature level of achievement than would be otherwise possible."[7] Unknown to either, the paths of Lionel Newsom and Central State had already begun to take similar turns.

Among his fellow faculty members at Morehouse was Dr. Martin Luther King, Jr., and Newsom and his family soon became more deeply involved in the struggle to integrate Atlanta. He helped jailed students to keep up with their studies and served as adviser to the activist Student Nonviolent Coordinating Committee. Then, in 1964, when he was only forty-five, he left Morehouse to accept the presidency of Barber-Scotia College—a small, black school in Concord, North Carolina. Only two years later, he resigned that post to take on what he believed to be the more important task of studying the role of the black college in general.

Was there a need for identifiably black colleges and universities in the nation's educational framework, and if so, how could they be sustained and developed? As associate director of the Institute for Higher Educational Opportunity in the South, he would help the Southern Regional Education Board to answer these questions. After two years of intensive investigation, the conclusion and findings were published in the book, *The Negro and Higher Education in the South,* which Newsom co-authored with Dr. James M. Godard. With the completion of this study, he had turned a personal conviction into a set of reliable theories— theories about how the higher education system works, or fails to work, for black students. He concluded:

> In order to ever have full integration in a society which has been divided for hundreds of years we must integrate equals—and in order to achieve equality many of our black students need an identification which gives them a security while it gives them a good education. Black students also need black models. For example, if they never see a black professor or black physician or a black college president or black engineers, they get the impression this is not possible. And they need to be proud of their black heritage, their black schools, all the while "running faster" to catch up by studying both cultures.[8]

Not surprisingly, Johnson C. Smith University and the city of Charlotte, North Carolina, lobbied hard to get and keep Newsom, but the challenge and opportunity of heading Central State beckoned. Just eighteen short months after they had chosen each other, Lionel Newsom and Central State would face the ultimate test—each would find out what the other was made of.

That ultimate test began on the inauspicious Wednesday morning of April 3, 1974. Catching the campus in mid-week, shortly after the resumption of classes following spring break, a massive tornado touched thirteen of the fourteen main campus buildings, demolishing nearly 70 percent of Central State's facilities, destroying irreplaceable documents, and claiming the lives of four members of the Central State family.

Polk Lafoon's book *Tornado* describes the erratic storm:

> It skinned all the land between town and the school, . . . crumpling the car in which Laura Lee Hull was on her way to see her mother, and killing Laura Lee. It picked up the truck that Ralph Smith, a Central State maintenance man, was driving, [and] killed him too. . . . The tornado came screeching across Scarborough House, traditional home of the president of Central State, and left the president's wife standing in the back hall while it brought the house down on top of her. . . . Galloway tower, the School's dominant landmark, met the wind with clock face, bells and a cornice set squarely atop it, like a mortarboard without the tassel. When the storm had passed, the mortarboard was gone. . . . It destroyed in short order Central State's credit union, killing its director, Evelyn Rockhold, in her car behind the building. . . . Survivors could see in a glance that virtually all their university was gone.[9]

The first priority was survival for the night, especially the care of the injured. Medical center doctors and nurses tended to victims in a first-aid station in the cafeteria because downed trees had blocked the routes of all emergency vehicles. Walter Bowie, a retired Army colonel who was then associate dean of students "brought," in Newsom's words, "all of his training to bear in every activity and became the executive officer."[10] Bowie organized student search and rescue parties. Then he and Newsom, along with Central's director of food services, Dorothy Chapman, set up a makeshift cafeteria to feed them and the other hungry, frightened students who were slowly emerging from their dormitory basements. Not until nearly midnight was a military unit from nearby Wright-Patterson Air Force Base able to clear the way for ambulances and Red Cross workers with water and food to reach the stricken campus.

Aerial view of the tornado destruction (looking north): Hallie Q. Brown Library is in center of photograph; the president's house is in foreground; Bundy Hall and Arnett Hall are to the right. (The first four tornado photos by Ohio Air National Guard; courtesy CSU Archives.)

Bundy Hall

Health Center

Hallie Q. Brown Library

Governor Gilligan visits campus to view tornado destruction. (Photo by E. Chamness.)

The following morning, Newsom charged Dean Wilson C. Jefferson, Jr. with arranging transportation home for all students. National Guardsmen cordoned off the campus buildings, while damage survey teams totalled up the physical losses. Bad as these were, everyone knew that the academic losses would be even greater if a plan could not be devised to resume classes, particularly for soon-to-graduate seniors. Perhaps an event such as this would be just the excuse that negative politicians needed to justify closing the school forever. True to his nature, Newsom made the bold stroke: on his calendar he penciled in April 16, a week from the following Monday, as the date to return seniors to their studies. The faculty concurred with one proviso—vice-president of academic affairs, Gus T. Ridgel, represented the feelings of many faculty members in requesting that *all* students be brought back on the sixteenth. Newsom was readily convinced. The student center and a few other small buildings could still be occupied; Wilberforce, Central's sister school, had been spared some classroom space that could be shared; and temporary, portable buildings could make up the difference. The plan worked. Thirteen hundred students returned. The Central State family now knew the true inner character of Lionel Hodge Newsom, and Newsom had learned a lot about the strength and resiliency of the school he was charged to govern. With everyone—students, professors, administrators, and government officials—working together, Central State would survive.

Exactly what role the State of Ohio would play in Central State's survival was far from certain at the beginning. Governor Gilligan had initially toured the broken campus before students were sent home and assured them, "I just came here to say stay cool and that Central State is going to live and serve Ohio for a long time to come." But later, back in Columbus, the governor told a press conference, "it is too soon to say if the money—$75 million and maybe even $100 million—can be found." Admitting that the final decision on rebuilding rested, in fact, not with him but with the Board of Regents and the Ohio General Assembly, he added that they would have to consider "not one institution, but the entire system of higher education in Ohio."[11]

Newsom quickly moved to answer the governor's doubts with a public statement that received national attention:

> Either pay the cost now as an investment or pay it later in destruction. We subsidize railroads, airplanes, every damn thing in the United States, and when we talk about a few more dollars to subsidize a black person it's not realistic. Central State is one of only two institutions in Ohio that black people control and where they are free to be models of leadership. Read Marx and some of the other revolutionaries and then find out how important it is for the U.S. to provide an opportunity to get blacks out of the ghetto.[12]

President Richard Nixon and his staff were certainly used to hearing such angry news releases from colleges, but not from a generally soft-spoken college president. On April 9, President Nixon, too, had toured the campus. Now he ordered federal disaster officials to "cut red tape to the bone."[13]

Within days the governor had revised his position back to his original optimistic support. Dolph Norton, chancellor of the Ohio State Board of Regents also reassured the school: "We are going to make certain that every student attending Central State University can finish his education as a Central State student. We will take a good look at what needs to be done in the future, and it's going to be done."[14] What Norton may have been implying was that the "good look" would make evident what everyone had long known: many renovations were sorely needed before the tornado struck. This was the opportunity to make them.

Returning students polled by the campus newspaper were far less reticent about pointing out the silver lining they saw around the cloud. Donna Scearce, a history major from Dayton said, "It's a shame that it takes a crisis to unite us; although it is good that [we] are finally waking up and trying to help each other." Reginald Harris, a sophomore majoring in industrial technology declared bluntly, "One good thing was that people who didn't know that CSU was on the map know now. Personally, I thought it was about time that CSU got some new buildings." A more thoughtful sociology senior, Arlene T. Vann, set the disaster in a realistic context that administrators and faculty were unwilling to voice:

> Central had plans to rebuild itself culturally and intellectually through physical expansions of buildings and programs. However, financing such programs has been a problem, especially since we are a predominantly black state school. The tornado came right on time, because now money is being appropriated for Central State to rebuild and expand. Central is fortunate, the greatest casualties were in buildings rather than people. Nothing can compensate for lives, but the tornado was God sent.[15]

The cleanup and rebuilding began immediately, but it did not proceed as fast as had been hoped. One reason for the delay was the state's policy of providing "self-insurance" on its university buildings—that is, if a university structure is destroyed, the legislature simply absorbs the cost of replacement through the general fund. This plan, however, could not cover a loss of such major proportions in a single year. Since no outside insurance had been purchased, the state had no set dollar value that it could refer to when requesting federal aid.

Central State's administration further compounded the delay—although to good result—by choosing "flexible funding" as opposed to "categorical grants." Categorical grants, familiar to everyone, would have provided 100-percent refunds, but they specified that existing, damaged buildings be repaired or replaced. Flexible funding reimbursed only 90 percent, but could be used for any building directly related to the campus. In retrospect, Newsom was glad to have made this choice, which carried with it "an opportunity to determine a more academically oriented philosophy . . . , [with] the library more or less in the center of the campus and all other buildings rotating around it—the hub of a wheel."[16] At that time, however, the additional delays brought about by the flexible funding plan disappointed many.

More disappointing still was the fact that while many students worked hard to pursue their studies and to help in the restoration, a significant minority seemed untouched by the needs of others. In the "Dean's Corner" segment of Central's *Gold Torch,* Dean Jefferson expressed his dismay at continued waste of short supplies; littering, vandalism, and looting; harmful and degrading hazing parties at fraternities and sororities; obscene displays during Mother's Day weekend; and the student apathy toward the rebuilding effort, both on campus and in nearby Xenia. Jefferson chided them: "Persons from around the nation have been giving of their time, of their money, of themselves, for the benefit of students at Central State. We give them thanks by trying to revert Central State to the street." He exhorted them, "Respect yourself for if you do not, no one else will."

Fortunately many students as well as a vast array of outsiders did have respect for Central State University. The following September, 1974, all but forty-one of the students expected to return did so. President Hollis A. Moore of Bowling Green State University saluted Newsom with an honorary doctorate, in March 1975, calling him, "the pilot who has weathered the storm." "We speak not only of tornadoes," Moore declared, "but lengths of concourse. You have wrestled the whirlwind and you have won."[17]

Indeed, the years succeeding the tornado saw the university's fortunes on a steadily upward curve. Previously established programs grew and prospered. An outstanding example of this was the summer Upward Bound program. Begun in 1966 as one of dozens of federal aid to minority programs encompassed in Lyndon Johnson's War on Poverty, the program provided over one hundred high school students a chance to escape their ghetto homes for six weeks of basic skills and cultural instruction and self-esteem exercises. The September 1975 *Alumni Journal* featured a brief history of the program's growth under the guidance of history professor Joseph D. Lewis, who had directed it since 1968. Asked to describe the program, Lewis said, "We try to show the young people that we care. We try to motivate them educationally and give them some direction in life." But he admitted that "a lot of people think that all we do all summer is shoot the ball and run"[18]—a reference to the sports element ever present in Upward Bound. Just two years later, the *Journal* proudly reported the "most spectacular strides in growth [gradewise] in

Paul Robeson Hall, built on site of Arnett Hall, Bundy Hall, Lee Hall, and old Jenkins Hall.

Walker Gym, first building to be constructed following tornado. (Photo by E. Chamness.)

the history of Upward Bound. The average grade level increase was 1.9 overall for learning skills development in Reading, Writing, Math and Science."[19]

100

Old Galloway Tower and new Alumni headquarters.

Benjamin Banneker Science Hall (1950), named in honor of Benjamin Banneker, first Negro-American scientist (1731–1806), is a three-story concrete building. It houses the Natural Sciences and Mathematics. This building has fourteen student laboratories, six research laboratories, a dark room, an animal room, library, departmental offices, classrooms and an elevated auditorium which seats 120. Audio-visual aids equipment are located in this auditorium for classroom aids in instruction. (Photo by E. Chamness.)

Jenkins Hall (Photo by E. Chamness.)

Lionel H. Newsom Administration Building was built on the site of the new Hallie Q. Brown Library that had been destroyed by the tornado. (Photo by E. Chamness.)

The Upward Bound Program also served as one of many recruitment tools utilized throughout the 1970s. In the second half of the decade, colleges and universities everywhere had begun to view with some alarm the nation's shifting demography. Census figures pointed to an ever declining percentage of Americans in the 18- to 22-year-old category from which the bulk of undergraduate enrollment had always been drawn. By the 1976–77 academic year, Central's enrollment had already dropped from the 2,500 level of 1970 to 2,260. At the request of the board of trustees, Newsom scheduled an all-day seminar at which he and approximately seventy-five other members of the CSU family were addressed by Dr. Gerald Parker, executive director of the Office of Enrollment Policy and Educational Research at the University of Cincinnati, and Sherman Jones of the Academy for Educational Development. Newsom concurred with these experts that the university must stabilize and then increase to a goal of 3,000 to 3,500 students. Parker advised that

> while full-time students will remain to be the most important, other programs such as international education; programs for adults, women and all minorities; and special or irregularly scheduled programs for specific populations can off-set projected losses and be the cushion needed to remain solvent.[20]

103

It should also be remembered that historically black colleges faced additional enrollment challenges in the late 1970s. National inflation and unemployment were on the rise—hitting hardest families at the lower end of the income spectrum and recently promoted minorities, who usually were the first to lose their jobs. These tandem economic problems also affected gifts from corporations, alumni, and foundations which traditionally have paid for the desirable extras that all universities convert into enrollment inducements. Further, federal government institution of a computerized editing program for Basic Educational Opportunity Grant (BEOG) applications resulted in delays and confusion regarding eligibility. Total BEOG, SEOG, Pell, and College Work Study monies were also reduced, and the guaranteed student loan program began to penalize colleges and universities in an effort to stem the growing tide of defaults. At Central State, where about 90 percent of students depended upon one of several kinds of financial aid, the results of this national turmoil were greatly amplified.

Yet despite these odds, Newsom and his faculty mobilized to fight declining enrollment and, for a time, succeeded. During the 1978–79 school year, while enrollment at the nation's black colleges dropped six times faster than the national average, Central State's rose by a healthy 9 percent. More than twenty-four hundred students attended that year. To what could the gain be attributed?

In the fall of 1979, Dean Edward L. Wingard of the College of Education analyzed the success factors for the Alumni Association. First, he credited a greater overall involvement in the recruitment effort. Attracting visitors—especially potential students—to the campus became everyone's job. Teams composed of faculty, staff, administrators, and students made appearances at the high schools. "University choirs, orchestra, athletic teams, student government, clubs, and other groups combined to publicize Central State University." The university's alumni associations in several cities as well as the national unit also became more actively involved in the campaign for increased enrollment.

As the experts had predicted, however, special programs proved to be the most significant improvements. According to Wingard:

> An Indispensable Skills Program was designed, funded, and implemented in 1977 to enhance the retention of students. This program focused on strengthening the basic skills of students in mathematics, reading, writing, and language skills. A diligent committee of faculty persons revamped the advising system of the University, thereby insuring improved academic advising of students. Under the

leadership of the Vice-President For Academic Affairs [Arthur E. Thomas] and with the support of the Faculty Senate, a weekly convocation period was scheduled that featured a host of outstanding scholars, lecturers, legislators, and educators each Tuesday of the academic year.[21] A number of other programs and activities were sponsored throughout the year by various groups at the University.[22]

Although Wingard's statement does not say so directly, in retrospect, one of Newsom's most valuable contribution after helping Central to rebound from the tornado was his selection of Dr. Arthur E. Thomas, a 1962 graduate of Central State, to fulfill the duties of the vice-president for academic affairs. Newsom's willingness to delegate to Thomas genuine power and authority, to allow him to work on independent projects, and to accept and acknowledge the glory that would accrue to Thomas was a great boost for the school. While past vice-presidents had largely carried out a supportive, background role, Newsom had Thomas work on projects of major importance and the young administrator quickly developed a high profile on campus and off.

In the fall of 1978, for example, it was Thomas who created both the official and unofficial linkages with Cincinnati's Urban Education Pilot Project under which Central State "adopted" Cincinnati's Hughes High School, its two junior highs, and its fifteen feeder elementary schools. Thomas's experience in public school education and his abilities as a speaker made him a logical choice to head the project which encompassed in-service training programs for teachers, academic encouragement programs for students, and placement and recruitment opportunities for Central State.[23] In February, the university received official notification that accreditation had been continued until 1988–89. The accreditation evaluation team cited nine areas of strength and seven areas of concern, but added that while the areas of concern were important, they were to a great extent already recognized by faculty, students, and administrators, and steps were already under way to ameliorate them.

The areas of strength were the following:

—The mission of Central State University is clearly stated and appears to be supported by the board of trustees and a majority of the campus community.
—There are many well-trained and dedicated faculty members who are working diligently to provide high quality instructional and educational experiences and carry-out the mission of Central State University.
—There is, in general, a working atmosphere characterized by understanding, commitment, orderliness, and business-like procedures.

—There is a sensitiveness among the administrative staff to the importance of planning, both short-range and long-range, and support for the institution of a method of accountability. This includes the effort being made to inaugurate a consistent, systematic data base.

—The top level administrators have a sensitivity to the importance of wholesome community relations and a commitment to the promotion of such relations.

—There appears to be a cooperative, positive working relationship between the staff of the Ohio Board of Regents, i.e., the state-wide coordinating agency for post secondary education, and administration of Central State University.

—Central State University officials perceive the need to pursue professional accreditation.

—There are several academic instructional and support areas which are notably strong and capable of making significant contributions to the students of Central State University. Among these are business administration, the physical and biological sciences, and the Indispensable Skills Program.

—The recent progress of the Office of Student Personnel Services in developing a consistent, unified team approach to serving students is a positive move and should continue.

Areas of concern pointed out were the following:

—There does not appear to be an adequate method of keeping the curriculum focused on the educational objectives, leading to course proliferation in some areas.

—Since one of the principal missions of the institution is to serve students who have achieved below average, the University should have better instruments to measure student progress.

—There is need for the professional counseling staff to work with students in non-academic, personal counseling.

—There is a difference in the perceptions of the administration, the Board of Trustees, and of a significant number of faculty members as to whether or not due process is being followed in the determination of faculty contract matters.

—There is the need that Central State University plan, interpret, execute, and monitor its Advanced Institutional Development Program in such a manner as to receive maximum benefit, including a heavy positive residual when Federal funds have been exhausted.

—There is a need to review and refine the University organization with regard to institutional research, facilities planning and physical plant services.

The "consistent, systematic data base" referred to in the list of strengths had begun to be implemented with the January 1979 introduction of the Higher Education Planning System (HEPS), a computerized system consolidating evaluation, budgeting, management, and planning. By providing in-service training to all employees, Newsom hoped to acquire more "timely and accurate" data for more informed decision making and better resource management within the university, as well as improved reporting to the board of trustees and the Ohio legislature. Here again, Newsom "assigned responsibility for initiating the HEPS program to Dr. Arthur E. Thomas."[24]

Another bright new star on Central State's horizon that had risen even further at the time of reaccreditation was the Indispensable Skills Program. As detailed in the 1978–79 brochure, "The New Central State University," the Indispensable Skills Program combines an "Instructional Component" with a "Special Student Assistance Component." Through the Instructional Component, at-risk, first-year students enroll in a full-year reading program, where their reading competencies and vocational decision-making capacities are carefully monitored. At the same time, they progress at their own pace sequentially through the required English and mathematics courses until they achieve a grade of "C" or better in all of them. The Special Student Assistance Component supports and reinforces the academic program through "tutorial services, seminars and workshops on academic and personal subjects . . . to assist students in acquiring those concepts and skills essential for growth and intellectual development."[25]

Perhaps the most admirable aspect of this truly "indispensable" program is the cooperation evident among several academic departments and the Communication Laboratory, the Electronic Multi-Media Center, the Human Relations Center, the Special Services Program, Upward Bound, and Veterans Upward Bound.

One exciting project that slowly materialized during the rebuilding years was the National Afro-American Museum and Cultural Center located on the old site of Wilberforce University. Some time after the 1947 church-state split, litigation over the property extending to O'Neill Hall was resolved and that land was deeded to Central State. It was the wish of the late W.O. Walker, a former Republican leader in state politics and the publisher of Ohio's largest black newspaper, that the animosity between the schools should be resolved and that the museum should be the link binding them together in spirit. Former Governor James Rhodes, a friend of Walker, worked diligently with Central State officials and others on the national level to see Walker's dream become a reality. In 1968, Congressman Clarence J. Brown of Urbana introduced the idea to the U.S. Congress. Planning began in earnest in 1972 when the Ohio legislature passed a bill introduced by State Representative C.J. McLin of Dayton.

McLin, too, had long been a champion of education and of the special needs of black Ohioans. Subsequently, he and the project's other proponents were able to influence the U.S. Congress to approve the creation of a fifteen-person commission to study the project, and the commission was first named in 1978 by President Jimmy Carter. At that point, the project seemed to lose momentum, but, in the spring of 1978, Congress directed the National Park Service to do a detailed on-site study.

However, the project was once again stalled: the Park Service was critical of the location in several respects. First, it found no firm evidence that Wilberforce had been a stop on the "underground railroad" used by escaping Southern slaves. Second, it found public support services—transportation, water and sewage, and fire protection—to be inadequate. Finally, it was critical of the absence of tourist accommodations such as hotels and restaurants. Fortunately, the university and the community had many advocates ready to respond. U.S. Congressman Clarence Brown was able to produce maps and other historical documents which the Park Service search had not discovered. Xenia City and Greene County officials reaffirmed their commitment to provide expanded sanitation and safety services. To the final criticism, the museum's backers—notable among them, members of the Central State University Alumni Association—replied that the building of tourist facilities, many of them black-owned small businesses, should result from the building of the museum, not precede it. At last the Park Service was convinced.

In September 1978, Central's Board of Trustees reported its selection of architects to the Ohio Department of Administrative Services in anticipation of the Park Service's final, official report. When, in January 1979, it was finally published, the picture it painted of the museum's impact on the area was even more favorable than had been anticipated. The study indicated that, in addition to its obvious cultural benefits, it could be expected to bring as much as $2.1 million and 200 to 400 new jobs to Greene County. All this was good news to the increasingly financially troubled university.

April 1981 marked the final site selection and purchase of land, and on November 23, 1982, an impressive ground-breaking ceremony celebrated the official beginning of construction. Director of the project, John Fleming, estimated that construction and exhibit costs for the 32,000 square-foot Phase I building would amount to approximately $4.5 million.[26]

By early 1980, Newsom and Thomas were able to progress one step further with their goal to improve resource management and to increase student academic achievement. They jointly announced the receipt of a

$1.5 million Strengthening Developing Institution Program (SDIP) grant from the federal government. Fortunately, this new grant money, unlike many grants, allowed for expenditures that would expand and reinforce projects already underway, as well as those which were in the planning or pilot phase. Established programs which received a new infusion of dollars included the HEPS management system, the Indispensable Skills Program, and the linkage between the weekly convocation series and Thomas's syndicated television program, "Like It Is."

In addition, Central State initiated an innovative program in cooperation with the Educational Testing Service of Princeton, New Jersey, for the purpose of enhancing students' "test sophistication." The plan included the administration of "mock tests" simulating such popularly required standard tests as the Graduate Record Examination (GRE), Law School Admission Test (LSAT), Medical College Admission Test (MCAT), and Business Management Admission Test (BMAT). The practice testing in conjunction with faculty-student discussion groups became available not only to seniors, but to juniors and even sophomores wanting to increase their competitive edge in gaining admission to graduate or professional programs.[27]

As with most of the improvements made during these rebuilding years, the ultimate goal of the testing program was to attract and retain undergraduates. Most higher education administrators would agree that while academic prestige is important, continued success in recruiting undergraduates depends also on achieving broad recognition in some extracurricular area. Since 1976, "Like It Is" had been a big drawing card for Central State. In the first four years of its existence, the show had gone from a local access community program to one that was nationally syndicated in more than fifty cities through the Central Educational Television Network. And in 1980, in an unusual cooperative effort between public and commercial television, commercial station WHIO-TV 7 in Dayton picked up broadcast rights as well.

The nature and format of the show made it an ideal project for the university because it could reap the benefits of "Like It Is" in two ways. Black leaders who might have hesitated to add a convocation address to their already busy schedules were lured by the prospect of consolidating the live speech and the taped television interview into one trip. Thus the program became a "recruiting tool" for guest lecturers as well as for prospective students—a showcase for Central State's uniqueness. Two years later, in 1982, Thomas's "Like It Is" took another major step forward. The Detroit, Michigan public school system selected the book—in which over a dozen selected interviews from the program are transcribed—as a supplemental reading text for their eleventh-grade American History classes. This prompted the publisher, Elsevier-Dutton Publishing Company of New York, to initiate a second printing.[28]

Other projects also showed Central successfully drawing on its special strengths to build and grow. In January 1982, it was one of only five institutions nationwide to be selected to assist the U.S. Department of Transportation in improving minority participation in contract and grant programs. In announcing the award of $100,000 in grants to the five schools, Dr. Melvin Humphrey, director of the Office of Small and Disadvantaged Business Utilization, said that the network would "coordinate the performance of transportation research, development and engineering tasks." Dr. Joseph Anthony served as project manager for the DOT project.

Similarly, in the spring of 1981, the university received a small grant of $10,000 from the International Communication Agency in Washington, D.C., which would benefit the Department of Foreign Languages and the International Studies Committee. Dr. William Felker, language department chairperson, stated that in addition to allowing nine students to complete a full quarter of study abroad, the grant would support a campus international festival. Benefits of this project also extended beyond the department and the individual students because the students participated in a "debriefing seminar and a series of discussions open to the university and the general public to make personal information about the foreign experience" available to the entire community.[29]

The autumn of 1982 again found Newsom expressing appreciation to his vice president for a project well done. Newsom said in a *Gold Torch* interview that "The energy, conviction, and commitment of Dr. Thomas were critical factors in sustaining momentum" on the preliminary development of a new language learning system. Tested in a series of seminars at Central State, the curriculum used the goal of constructing a foundation of attitudes and understanding of language for students who had previously been slated for more traditional remediation.

As the first half of this decade drew to a close, Central also experienced some improvement in its enrollment picture. Although still down from its 1978 figure, the 1983–84 totals showed twenty more students than the 1982–83 roster. More importantly, the Full-Time Equivalent enrollment (FTE) had actually improved by ninety-seven over the previous year, resulting in a greater potential for state subsidy. Director of admissions Edith Johnson, pointing out that the availability of financial aid is always a key factor in enrollment size, reminded the university once again that retention is a bigger job than initial recruitment. In fact, the school could take particular pride in even a small increase in light of the national statistics showing a decline during this decade in the percentage of college-bound students who were black.[30]

Unfortunately, not all of the news emanating from Central State University in the early 1980s was good news. Most of the problems that arose were financial. Budget cuts and fee increases were attempted with limited success, and Newsom soon found himself devoting almost all his time to the school's financial difficulties.

As 1981 arrived, Newsom found himself penning a rather disheartening open letter to the Central State family, touching on the most salient factors in the general economic downturn. He quoted outgoing Governor James Rhodes's statement that "Ohio is the victim of the economic blizzard that is rampaging across the country . . . taking its toll in human misery in every part of our State. The chilling effects of high interest rates and inflation have left tens of thousands of Ohioans without jobs this year."

"Who could have predicted," Newsom wondered rhetorically, "we would be facing 20 per cent interest rates, 13 per cent inflation, and 9 1/2 per cent unemployment in Ohio?" With the state paying out over one billion dollars in unemployment benefits and over $300 million in welfare payments in 1980 alone, it was not surprising that other budget areas— among them education—should have to suffer. All state-assisted institutions enacted fee increases to offset the 7-percent shortfall from the state, and another round of fee raises and cuts was anticipated.

Newsom minced no words in interpreting what the 7-percent, half-million dollar cut would mean at Central State:

> This has increased our financial difficulties and simultaneously imposed new and heavier burdens on all of us. More significantly, it means the University is unable to pay many of its debts, must cut supplies, cannot purchase new and needed equipment, must refuse to hire additional personnel, and if possible, not replace a few present employees, reduce all expenditures except those that are fixed by contracts, and give careful consideration to abolishing some programs and merging others. We must give careful study to our use of water and other energy resources, telephone equipment and usage, increasing teaching loads and the use of qualified administrators in the classroom.

He also revealed in this same interview that in December 1980 only eleventh-hour efforts on the part of the Board of Trustees had enabled the school to meet its payroll, but he warned, "If it happens again, the University will be unable to pay because Central State has no endowment, nor money reserves."[31]

The austerity measures which he outlined to meet this grave situation would touch everyone.

> All of us can help if we do more for ourselves: turn off lights not in use, reduce lighting to only that which is necessary to see, reduce telephoning both locally and long distance on University equipment, reduce travel to the necessary only, reduce overtime to only the essential, eliminate all waste and vandalism, reduce publications, printing, duplicating and mimeographing, and understand why certain University sports, programs and other non-essentials will be cut.

While the burden of many of these measures would weigh most heavily on faculty, administration, and staff, students too were pressed hard to alleviate the negative cash flow situation. Henceforth, student balances of $200 or more would result in the student's dismissal until the debt was paid. Further, students utilizing financial aid—and this was the case for the vast majority of those attending—were given greater responsibility and more serious consequences if their paperwork was not completed correctly and on time.[32]

Newsom concluded his letter with the most unpleasant news of all: while cutting deeply to meet their current shortfall, they must also plan for an anticipated second round of cuts for the following biennium.

Another source of the problem lay largely in Washington, D.C., where the policies of the Republican Reagan administration cut immediately and deeply into both institutional programs for higher education and personal help for students in the form of grants and loans. Not only were student programs such as Pell grants cut in total dollars, leaving many students without funds, but filing procedures and deadlines were altered arbitrarily, causing confusion and loss of financial aid even among students who were still eligible.

It soon became apparent, however, that many members of the university family, too, were part of the problem rather than part of the solution. A second open letter from the president published almost exactly one year after the previous one, stated that many areas of waste and abuse had not improved. Even some requests which had seemed both reasonable and relatively "painless" had not been complied with by many. One example was in on-campus correspondence: "we asked you to use inter-campus envelopes, to mimeograph and duplicate, where and when possible, on both sides of the paper. *Too many of us have failed to heed the warn-*

ing. "[33] In telephone communications, too, gross abuse continued. *"Unless there is more prudent use of telephones,"* Newsom warned, *"it will be necessary for us to either disconnect those telephones where there are violations, or charge violators personally for abuse."*

This time, compliance would not rely on the honor system; beginning with spring semester, 1982, departmental printing and graphic services would be reviewed for approval before work began. Calls would be monitored for caller, time, and destination, so that patterns of abuse could be spotted and rectified. But the most serious and costly violations of Newsom's 1981 edict had been in the readmission of students with overdue fee balances. "Some faculty members," he revealed, "harmed both themselves and the University by allowing students to attend classes who had not paid their fees or finished the registration process."[34] Within a few months, the board of trustees had responded to the escalating internal and external financial woes by instituting another fee increase—a necessary move, but one almost assured to hasten the previous years' enrollment decline.[35]

Nor were all of Central State's problems in the early 1980s financial ones. During the 1980–81 academic year, an investigative team of the Office of Civil Rights, U.S. Department of Education, visited six state-assisted higher education institutions in Ohio, including Central State. Their review, reported in the spring of 1981, revealed that although the State of Ohio had made improvements in providing access to higher education for black students, it was nevertheless in violation of Title VI of the 1964 Civil Rights Act. The finding was based specifically on the state's maintenance of Central State "as an institution for blacks" and the state's actions which "dissuaded white students from choosing to attend Central State."

Newsom, again in an open letter to *The Gold Torch,* quoted the three central points in the Office of Civil Rights' report:

1) Racial identifiability of student enrollment at this and other institutions. Blacks represented 80.5 per cent of Central State University's enrollment in the Fall of 1980, 2 per cent at Miami University and 6.9 at Wright State University.
2) Racial identifiability of faculty, administrators, and boards of trustees at this and other institutions. Central State University employed 17.3 percent of black faculty in Ohio, and 20.1 per cent of the system's black administrators.
3) Failure to enhance Central State by providing fewer and lesser quality resources, and by duplicating Central State University's programs at other nearby State institutions.[36]

While he and others connected with the university consistently reminded all who would listen that none of the findings suggested wrongdoing on the part of Central State, or its administrators, the Ohio media often failed to emphasize this distinction.

Governor James Rhodes involved himself directly in the issue, attempting to redirect the negativism of the media by bringing to light the unresponsiveness of the U.S. Department of Education to Ohio's request for further negotiations. Jim Ripley reported on February 9, 1982, in the *Dayton Daily News* that the governor's position remained that "the racial identifiability of Central State University in itself violates no statute . . . and that the unique educational mission of that institution actually has enhanced . . . the opportunities of educationally disadvantaged students in a way that is fully consistent with nationally acknowledged principles of affirmative action." Furthermore, Rhodes argued that the statistics could be viewed in an entirely different light: "92.9 percent of all black students in Ohio attend institutions other than Central State University."[37]

For awhile it might have been hoped that these external troubles would help reunite the Central State family much as the tornado had done several years earlier. Indeed, alumni president James Farmer attempted this type of rally in his opening letter to his fellow Centralians when the issue first broke in 1981. "While the State of Ohio is working on its answers for years of INEQUITY to Central State, let's work on sharing a little of our EQUITY with our alma mater," wrote Farmer.[38] Ultimately, however, all recognized that the amounts of money to be raised by even a very successful alumni drive would fall short of making up the deficits in the school's day-to-day operating expenses.

By spring of 1984, the financial woes had begun to have a serious effect on student as well as faculty morale. Newsom attempted to answer some of the students' concerns by offering to participate in an hour-long forum conducted by business students Marquita Forte and Keith Lymore. He quickly diffused some of the students' complaints by pointing out that CSU was merely implementing "new" policies that had been standard operating procedure at other state schools all along.

Question: Why can't a student who receives financial aid and is due a refund at the end of each quarter get a bookslip if they have enough money coming to their account to cover the balance of the purchase of books with the credit slip?

Answer: A student with this problem still cannot obtain a bookslip because it is covered by government money that is not available until the end of the quarter. At other universities (Ohio State for example) there is no bookslip policy.

In response to other questions, Newsom pointed out that the students had simply failed to apprise themselves of rule changes printed in the student catalog, and that they had to accept more responsibility for cutting waste and other abuses. He also reminded them that rather than being "top heavy with employees in the administration building" as the students had suggested, Central Stage had fewer personnel in most administrative roles than other similar institutions, and that there had been three staff reductions during his tenure in office.[39]

Assistant business manager Tekeste B. Abraham similarly attempted to allay students' fears and dissatisfactions by granting an interview to a student newspaper reporter. Abraham cited the now familiar list of factors responsible for the deficit: too few in-state students, non-self-supporting auxiliary services, high utility costs, and high per capita costs of physical operations due to the fact that enrollment never approximated the planned-for 5,000 students. But ultimately, his answers, too, would focus on the students' need to share the burdens and inconveniences. Later in April, the pressures of the business office were made abundantly apparent: Business Manager Ralph Sheppard suffered a mild heart attack while in his office.

Clearly, the financial situation at the university was beginning to take its toll on everyone. It had also become clear to President Newsom that it was time to entrust his beloved Central State to the hand of another; he announced to the Board of Trustees his intention to retire.

Paraphrasing the third chapter of Ecclesiastes, Newsom informed the board that "both logic and chronology compel me to write this letter seeking your approval of my request to retire at the close of the last day of January, 1985, for I feel it will be in the proper season and at the right time." "I can leave," he continued, "with the sacred belief that my wife and I have given Central State—my school—no less than 100 per cent on all occasions."[40] It was evident from the many accolades written and spoken during his last months in office, that many of his colleagues agreed.

six

The Central State University Family

In setting forth guidelines for institutions of higher education and for those persons whose task it is to assess the quality of such institutions, the North Central Association of Colleges and Secondary Schools stresses that "institutions of higher education serve a variety of purposes [and] . . . it is important that each institution clearly determine the particular tasks to which it will commit its resources."[1] The *Guide* goes on to say that each school "should give consideration to its role in the immediate geographical community, in the nation, and in the international community," and should then formulate its unique plan for fulfilling these roles. Clearly, Central State, throughout its existence, conceived of itself as more than a purveyor of information and skills leading to certain degrees and professional certifications. Harry G. Johns sums it up this way: "Deep concern for students and desire to assist them took on a surrogate family role and touched every aspect of a student's life."[2] The purpose of this chapter, then, will be to examine this familial infrastructure: the ways in which it has manifested itself in campus life, its possible origin, and its success.

The major characteristics of the familial infrastructure are: close personal relationships among students, faculty, and administrators, often lasting beyond their campus association; concern for keeping disagreements within "the family" while presenting a united position to the outside world; willingness of individuals or groups to make sacrifices for one another; the relevancy of student life to the educational task and the amount and quality of student participation in extracurricular activities, especially student government; policies and practices that foster high faculty morale, including significant participation in decision-making; and, of course, loyalty, interdependability, and cooperation. Although several of these factors were firmly established at Central State/Wilberforce even before the time of Charles Wesley's arrival, the two-decade impact of his personality and leadership style resulted in a strengthening and expansion of this familial infrastructure. Subsequent administrators sought, to a greater or lesser extent, to maintain elements of this family-like atmosphere in spite of overwhelming and irreversible changes in American higher education as well as in the structure of the American family.

With this in mind, the success of this system will be assessed by four criteria: student achievement, the record of distinguished alumni, continuous alumni support of the institution, and the number of students drawn from the families of the school's alumni.

One of the most obvious indicators of the "spirit of enterprise and cooperation,"[3] noted by one careful observer of the Central State campus, was the close personal relationships among students, faculty, and administrators. Evidence of this are numerous and varied; three examples will suffice. The first is a reminder to students, set forth in the 1959 "Student Handbook," about chaperones at student parties:

> Please remember that the chaperones are your guests. . . . Chaperones should be made to feel a part of the group. Do not isolate them in a "chaperone corner." . . . At a buffet dinner see that someone relieves chaperones of their dishes when they are finished. At the dance it is proper and fitting to have some couples exchange dances with the chaperones. The man should ask permission of the man and then ask his lady for the dance. The gentleman chaperone will then invite the other man's date for the dance. . . . Where games or other activities take place, be sure to invite the chaperones to participate.

Such courtly, traditional good manners may not, of course, have been in practice at every campus event, but the assumption of anything approximating this level of faculty involvement at a student party is worth noting. The advice has an unmistakably parental ring to it that was unusual in college life even in 1959.

A more modern example may be found in a brief address by Dr. Wesley on the occasion of the opening of the college's first student union in March 1964. He believed that the building of the union represented a place where administration, faculty, alumni, students, and friends would have the opportunity of meeting and associating informally with one another. He stressed that while there were facilities for "fun and play," such as bowling alleys and billiard rooms, the union would also be a center for

117

more educational pursuits, such as lectures and dramatic presentations, and for "correct dining, pleasant association and profitable conversation," not unlike the atmosphere that might prevail in the dining room of a good home. Wesley continued: "Freedom from home and its regulations is one of the steps that must be taken by those who are growing up. . . . Such activity and freedom require responsibility and ability to make choices. . . . The College Center should become a place where freedom can be learned under direction and guidance and in a good atmosphere."[4] Clearly, the faculty and administrators were expected to do more than teach a body of knowledge and organize the curriculum. They were also expected to guide and assist the students in the much more fundamental tasks of becoming adults.

The attempt to convey instruction and guidance in a warm, home-like environment is still evidenced in individual mentor-protégé relationships between faculty members and students. But while much of the communication between the university and its children has become more official, vestiges of the old ways remain in some aspects of campus life. In the spring of 1979, for example, the Special Services program added a Career Resource Library in Simpson Hall. Althenia Morrow, counseling coordinator, pointed out that its setting was a "small, serene lounge where students (faculty and staff) may use a variety of career information materials."[5] Thus Central was demonstrating sooner than many colleges that it felt a responsibility for helping students view their education in the context of the world of work. This sensitive, personalized counseling outreach provided a much needed supplement to the typical placement office services.

There are several other causes of the intimacy among various groups at Central State. One of these was a student personnel program instituted during Wesley's administration that provided faculty members with data they needed to understand students' strengths, weaknesses, and probable needs. Richard Kidd, a faculty member for many years, talked of this in his 1959 study, "Problems Encountered by the Faculty of Central State College, Wilberforce, Ohio." Kidd found that

> the counseling program at the College is an integral part of the instructional program and seeks a high degree of coordination between the student personnel department and individual teachers. As a basis for instruction and counseling, every teacher has access to student personnel data. These findings indicate that the coordination between individual faculty members and the student personnel

department with regard to policies and practices pertaining to admissions, counseling, and testing parallel satisfactorily the best thought [i.e., scholarly theory] in student personnel services.

This tradition has advanced and expanded through a strong Academic Foundations Program and, most recently, new and better instruments to measure student progress. An important element in Central State's Academic Foundations Program has been the attempt to secure counselors and administrators who can relate on a personal level to disadvantaged students. Dorothy Boyer, counseling coordinator, told a student reporter in 1977 that her own high school counselor had labeled her "not college material"—a judgment that her master's degree from Rutgers University subsequently proved faulty. She expressed the opinion that "CSU gives the students a chance to make adjustments and get their program together, unlike many other colleges" with larger enrollments or more widely recognized names.[6]

Boyer's concerns, expressed in the same 1977 interview, that most students were not taking enough advantages of such specialized programs was echoed in the 1979 report of the North Central Association Evaluation Team. While they lauded "the recent progress of the Office of Student Personnel Services in developing a consistent, unified team approach to serving students," they pointed out the need for the professional counseling staff to work more with students in "non-academic, personal counseling." They also stated that "since one of the principal missions of the institution is to serve students who have achieved below average, the University should have better instruments to measure student progress."[7]

Under President Newsom and subsequently under President Thomas, the school has sought to embrace these proposals through, among other methods, the innovative assessment program funded under the 1980 Strengthening Developing Institutions grant obtained from the federal government.[8]

Kidd's study makes note of another feature of early campus life which also had an impact on interpersonal relationships: on-campus faculty residences. Mentioned by Kidd in the context of narrowing the salary differential suffered by Central State faculty in comparison with faculty at comparable schools, this housing was provided without charge to the teachers. Not all, but most, of the teaching staff during these years were accommodated in World War II barracks that had been remodeled for that purpose. As one long-time staff member, Mildred Henderson, put it:

> Everyone lived in the barracks like one big family—we all were one. We never missed a game; we had our own rooting section. . . . We always had beautiful Christmas dinners, the family in the community would have dinner with the students on campus. Students did not have to leave campus at that time—we were just one big family.[9]

No doubt the on-campus faculty residences led to camaraderie among the teachers, as well as between them and their students.

Regrettably, as times changed, the generation gap widened. Professor James T. Henry, who served all the school's chief executives from Wesley through Newsom, views the students of the 1940s and 50s as different in kind from those of later periods. These were "more mature students, strong willed students and students who wanted to get on with the *raison d'etre* of the institution."[10] As the student body began to look more to its peers than to its elders for moral codes and world perspective, relations between students and faculty became more formalized and undeniably more strained at times. Mentor-protege relationships between individual teachers and learners replaced the aggregate model. By 1974, only one on-campus faculty residence, containing six units, remained. Access to them was still sought after, but the patronage system used in their assignment frequently contributed to divisiveness among faculty members. Destroyed by the tornado, the structure was never replaced. From 1974 onward, only the university president has been provided with a residence.

It can be argued that the greatest factor influencing the early formation of the familial infrastructure was Charles H. Wesley's guidance and example. Like his teachers who shared their Christmas celebrations, Wesley was known to maintain "an open-door policy in his office and at home for students and faculty."[11] Harry Johns remembers:

> He [Wesley] cared about every aspect of a student's life, on or off campus. He felt that the faculty and administration existed primarily for the purpose of developing the talents of the young men and women who had entrusted their lives to our care. Therefore, the activities and decisions made by the administrative staff in the performance of their duties and in carrying out their responsibilities, were always in terms of what was in the best interest of the students. . . .
>
> This deep concern for students and the desire to assist them took on a surrogate family role and touched every aspect of a student's life. In a sense, the student body became one big family with many of the administrators taking on the role of parents that a number of students had never experienced. This sincere interest and concern gave to students a sense of self and confidence that many had never known.[12]

Through the strength of his own example—whether through an admiring desire to emulate or an embarrassment at falling short—Wesley motivated his teachers and fellow administrators to put student welfare first and to treat them as not-quite-adult children with a need for loving discipline.

As the reins of power were passed to much younger men, and as young people became increasingly sophisticated and "worldly," this image of Central State as a home altered somewhat. To a greater extent, as years went by, students related closely only to their peers and looked less to faculty and administrators as role models. Discipline, both academic and social, was called upon with increased frequency.

Whereas the familial spirit had once naturally filtered down to students' relations with each other and produced a constructive, enterprising campus environment, later administrators found it necessary to structure these student and faculty relationships. Relevancy of student life to the educational task of an institution is an important feature of the North Central Association's scheme of evaluation. The association asserts that it is "the responsibility on the part of the institution to concern itself with and to maximize the educational value of all aspects of a student's life on campus." Central State attempted to do this prior to 1969, both by limiting access to distracting or counterproductive activities, and by organizing and authorizing extracurricular activities of a high educational or moral value.

Again, we may examine the 1959 Student Handbook for an expression of the prevailing rules and regulations during the Wesley years. Dormitory living at this almost entirely residential school was, as the North Central *Guide* suggests, "under the supervision and . . . control of the institutional authorities, with appropriate student involvement in the determination and implementation of policy." Room keys were given out by the dormitory director of each building, and students were divided into three rotating committees, each with nine-week turns of duty in enforcing "Observance of Quiet Hours, Hall and Bathroom Conditions, and Room Cleanliness and Campus Conduct." Check-in time and hours for male visitors were stringently regulated in women's dormitories, and the list of privileges for senior women is an indicator of the restrictiveness practiced with younger female students. Identification of men leaving on dates, elaborate permission procedures for overnight absences or for riding in cars, and rules regarding off-campus housing were applied to female students during this era of double standards. But men also had to justify their requests for keeping a car on campus, had to meet a minimum grade point average to participate in clubs or organizations, had to present written absence excuses to classroom faculty, and had to abide by a list of "Basic Policies" which included prohibition of imbibing alcohol, gambling, profanity, and secret marriages, as well as more serious offenses.

President Groves quickly realized upon coming to the campus that conditions of behavior in the dormitories had slipped significantly during the early 1960s. He also comprehended that students would not readily accept a return to the role of dormitory directors as stiff disciplinarians. Rather, he proposed that they act as counselors or advisers who would "substitute reason and proper choice for pressure." He invited "younger faculty members, those unmarried and the married without children to take up residence in the dormitories as well, in hopes that their presence would encourage an atmosphere of intellect and would deter the vandalism and other undesirable behavior."[13] Mature, inner-directed students flourished under such new philosophies, but unfortunately many others floundered.

Warning signals were abundant. For example, prior to 1960, in spite of the fact that a cumulative grade point average of 2.0 had to be maintained, nearly all students participated actively in one or several campus organizations. Thus the situation at Central State closely paralleled the criterion of the North Central Association: ". . . a well-planned and well-executed program of extra-class activities broad enough to encompass a wide range of student interests. The participation of students in the activities program should be encouraged."[14] In addition to an extensive list of religious organizations mentioned in Chapter III, Central State offered literary and musical groups (The Players' Guide, The Humanities Collegium, The College Choir, Women's Glee Club, Men's Glee Club, The Concert Band, The Marching Band, and The Mixed Ensemble); departmental organizations (The Home Economics Club, The American Chemical Society, The Future Teachers of America, The Student Forum, and Future Business Leaders of America); and several miscellaneous special interest groups (the Women's Recreational Club, Cadet Officers Club, Oklahoma Club, and the International Relations Club). Most important to the formation and continuance of the familial spirit, however, were those inherently quasi-familial bodies—the fraternities and sororities.

For such a small school, Central State maintained chapters of a rather large number of Greek organizations, indeed, all those having an historically black membership. There were Alpha Phi Alpha and its sister sorority Alpha Kappa Alpha, Phi Beta Sigma and its sister Zeta Phi Beta, Omega Phi Psi and its sister Delta Sigma Theta, and Kappa Alpha Psi which did not have any sorority association. All of these fraternities, and to a slightly lesser extent the sororities, developed their unique memberships, appealing primarily to socializers, athletes, or "serious" scholars. No one with a grade point average below 2.5, however, was allowed to pledge—a fact which extended considerable pressure to study on sophomores looking toward their junior and senior years. While strenuous hazing was prohibited by the college, certain rigors and embarrassments were inevitably contrived, so a large service-oriented fraternity—Alpha Phi Omega—was instituted for those seeking a less demanding initiation. At the peak of fraternity/sorority involvement in the late 1950s, an average of 85 percent of junior and senior students were affiliated with one of these organizations. Many students were also a part of Greek honor societies such as Beta Kappa Chi, Phi Alpha Theta, and Alpha Kappa Mu, and Central State's strong Panhellenic Council set the tone for much of the campus's student life.

Strong as the Greek organizations were, they were not permitted total autonomy on campus. Former President Lewis A. Jackson recalls that during the years between 1950 and 1957 "some of the fraternities were evaluated [by Student Personnel Services] in accordance with good operating practices. Again improvements were made."[15]

After 1960, participation in extracurricular clubs and organizations sanctioned by colleges declined rapidly nationwide. Belonging to a group that had been approved by school officials was no longer "cool." In addition, at Central State an ever-growing number of students could not maintain required grade point levels—in fact, an alarming number were dropping out or being dismissed due to their failing grades. A study undertaken in 1969 by Frances H. Hawkins, registrar and director of admissions, found that of the 843 new freshmen admitted in 1964, only 226, or 27 percent, were able to graduate by the end of 1968.[16] President Branson and Vice President Woolfolk pointed to the need for special academic and motivational programs to reduce the attrition of high-risk, ill-prepared undergraduates. Many years would pass, however, before ideas such as the Indispensable Skills Program, developed under President Newsom, would bring these concerns to satisfactory outcomes.

Student government is another element of concern to the North Central Association system of evaluation. Although they concede that "the nature and extent of student participation in the making of decisions" may vary widely among successful institutions, they insist on the "major important that continuing systematic provision be made for the expression of student opinion . . . and that serious consideration" be given to it. The familial and, to a great extent, paternalistic nature of Wesley's tenure at Central

State might lead one to expect that student participation in decision making would be discouraged, but given the prevailing attitudes in this era before any national pressures for student rights, Central State provided a considerable forum for student opinion. The Student Council (executive officers including a president, vice-president, recording secretary, correspondent secretary and treasurer) and a Student Court shared the governing and advisory duties with six standing boards (Charities, Communications, Spirits and Tradition, Orientation, Organization, and Elections) and with the Men's Senate, the Association of Women Students, the Line Monitors Court, and all of the dormitory councils. Overall participation in student government, as in the fraternities and sororities, was extensive.

Paul McStallworth, a former professor, made this comment:

> A good index to the quality of student-faculty relationships may be revealed by the caliber of student government officials throughout the Wesley regime. As a former dean of students, I believe that the majority were on the honor roll, were leaders in their various campus activities and hardly any lost face by having to resign or undergo recall from student office. The operation of student court and the administration of justice were models of administration. It spoke well for the faculty advisers of the various classes, clubs and student organizations.[17]

But in the arena of student government, too, the calmer standards of the 1940s and 50s inevitably gave way to the turbulent ones of the 1960s and 70s. The Central State family was not what it used to be—but then, families themselves were experiencing rapid and often negative changes in their structure.

One professor, recalling the difference in student government leaders, commented that after the late 1940s "student leadership was as the wind blows." Yet, when asked whether student unrest on the CSU campus was different than elsewhere, he joked, "Within the proper context of the historic period of the 1960s the so-called riots at CSU were a field outing for the Shawnee Indian children."[18] Another often retold anecdote, substantiated by former President Branson, was his rejoinder to people who commented on Central's radicalism: "The theory of revolution is taught at Antioch College, but they have tried to move the laboratory work to Central."[19]

Nevertheless, it was also true that these tumultuous years were a crucible in which many strong student leaders were formed.

If we view the faculty and administrators as the parents of this Central State family, the students who led and set examples through student government posts must be seen as its big brothers and sisters, but ones who rose to their positions of authority not by the arbitrary fate of earlier birth, but by the democratic selection of their fellow students. As in real families, the "parents" of the 1960s and 70s were alarmed at the direction some of the brotherly and sisterly advice was taking.

What, then, did individual faculty members gain through their association with Central State—a school where the workload was often greater and the paycheck smaller than at other universities? The North Central Association *Guide* states emphatically that "high morale is essential to faculty effectiveness." It includes within the policies and practices with a bearing on faculty morale "salaries; service loads; provisions for retirement, insurance and other fringe benefits; and provision of office facilities, secretarial help, technical assistance, and student assistance," and discusses in another section, "recognition of good teaching; induction of new faculty members; faculty recruitment, retention, and promotion; opportunities for professional growth and development," and "[responsibility] for many decision-making activities."

Kidd, in his 1959 study of the faculty, looked at problems faced by them in several of these areas, including, "physical working conditions, professional growth, faculty welfare, instruction and student relations, and participation in policy-making and faculty personnel administration."

Certainly in the area of salary and other tangible benefits, Central State for many years fell below the levels offered by other schools. Indeed, one faculty member insists that they "never reached the height comparable to their sister schools." This was true at least until 1965, President Wesley sometimes giving to needy students dollars which might have been used to augment salaries. Kidd, too, found a number of teachers who complained of this differential between their pay and "those of teachers in other colleges or with workers in comparable professional groups." He concluded, however, that "notwithstanding the problem of low salaries encountered by teachers, the college has followed a consistent practice of raising salaries annually, thus attempting to alleviate the differential between its median salary and the national norm."

As noted previously, this goal was eventually reached in the early 1960s. Table 1 shows the salary schedule for all the teaching ranks for the years 1950 to 1985. It may be seen that while the overall figures remain low, the percentage of increase is substantial—approximately 7.7 percent per five year average for the highest rank and 7.4 percent per five year

125

average for instructors. Table 1 also indicates the significant incentive built into the system for encouraging teachers to obtain advanced degrees.

Thus, morale might be maintained even in the face of relatively low salaries by virtue of the appearance that conditions were constantly improving and by each teacher's awareness that he or she might attain a higher place on the pay scale through the individual effort of obtaining additional education. Also, the personal closeness of faculty and administrators makes it likely that most knew, as Paul McStallworth asserted, that "Central State seldom if ever received full and adequate state allocations for overall operations."

Finally, the chief administrators' attitudes throughout the years played a major role in boosting faculty morale in this regard. Professor Emeritus James T. Henry, Sr. stated that President Wesley "was intimately concerned about the quality and economic welfare of his faculty at a time [when] the faculty of this university was disgracefully underpaid in comparison to the other state institutions."[20]

It is an unfortunate fact that the lot of Central State's faculty did not steadily improve over the succeeding years. Ironically, the apex of faculty self-direction and satisfaction was probably achieved during the era of administrative instability that followed the Wesley years. To a varying extent, Presidents Groves, Branson, and Jackson pressed for greater faculty autonomy and prestige and argued forcefully that higher salaries were needed if Central was to attract the best scholars from elsewhere. As Dr. Oscar Woolfolk, then vice-president for academic affairs, pointed out in his 1969 address to the faculty, "There is no one in higher education today who is more mobile than the black Ph.D. We have been most fortunate at Central State to retain loyal, dedicated and highly qualified faculty members."[21] By the following spring, with additional monies available, the Board of Trustees was persuaded to adopt a new, more attractive salary range starting with an $8,000 base for instructors and reaching to $21,000 for full professors on the highest step.[22]

In the years following the 1974 tornado, however, priorities were redirected, though with the noble intention of paying first for budget items more obviously linked to students' welfare. President Newsom, himself a self-made man who valued and practiced self-sacrifice, expected faculty to serve the school as much out of devotion to their profession and to their black heritage as for monetary reward. Faculty member Henry feels that during these years the faculty bore an unfair distribution of the always limited state funds, and that the school was "unable to attract to its doors" scholars whose excellence in research and experimentation could

TABLE 1
Average Salaries for Central State University
1950–1985

Year	Professor	Associate Professor	Assistant Professor	Instructor
1950	4,000	3,300	2,820	2,700
1955	6,000	4,230	4,200	3,900
1960	8,625	7,550	6,400	5,200
1965	12,200	9,500	9,000	5,500
1970	15,159	13,164	11,135	8,851
1975	19,528	15,904	13,750	11,423
1980	23,962	18,818	15,925	13,429
1985	37,581	28,556	24,380	22,541

SOURCE: Figures obtained from the records of Catherine M. Cunningham, Central State University, Payroll Department, January 8, 1987.

have promoted growth. Sabbatical leaves, travel, and other amenities were virtually done away with during the austerity programs of the late 1970s and early 80s. Still, Henry admits that many dedicated teachers accepted these hardships—a fact that their "students will never forget."[23] The old pattern of faculty self-sacrifice was firmly rooted in CSU history.

Indeed, the need for equipment, materials, and supplies as well as the inadequacy of secretarial assistance proved even from the time of Kidd's study to be the most bothersome of problems faced by the faculty. It is interesting that the first of these, the difficulties with the instructional budget, was complained about more than either low salaries or the secretarial shortage—interesting because the former could really affect the student's welfare, while the latter would cause more personal hardship and inconvenience to the faculty. This supports the notion that the familial nature of the school was founded on a willingness for self-sacrifice. While Kidd found the matters of the instructional budget and lack of secretarial assistance to be legitimate concerns, he concluded that lack of funds rather than administrative failure was at fault. Hence, they were likely to have a lesser effect on faculty morale than if they had been seen as stemming from inadequate or incorrect procedures.

According to the North Central Association, schools may also be usefully evaluated by the official support structure which they offer their faculty in instructional planning and adaptation to the institution's practices and procedures, by their institutional concern for the improvement of instruction, and by their encouragement of academic freedom. In these areas, Central State's record seems to be a good one. Kidd discovered that in "orientation of new teachers, professional information services, professional faculty meetings and institutes, and participation on faculty committees commensurate with faculty interest and experiences . . . , the practices of the College compare favorably with the best administrative practices."

During the Wesley years, frequent faculty meetings were held for the purpose of inspiring faculty members and challenging them in regard to their roles of teaching young men and women. He also encouraged—or, perhaps more correctly, demanded—that his teachers and fellow administrators take advantage of the openness of the academic environment to engage in independent thought and action. Harry Johns recalls that "those who could not work independently or those who needed close supervision did not last very long."

A major factor, then, in the level of morale of the Central State faculty was the high regard they observed for personal and professional growth. According to Kidd's research, "when the criteria and practices [pertaining to advancement and personal recognition] are compared with the best thought, it appears that those of Central State College meet satisfactorily those recommended in the professional literature on college and university administration."

Wesley certainly set an early example as a primary motivator in both recognition and advancement rewards for professional development. According to Walter Sellers, "Dr. Wesley encouraged and assisted faculty members in their efforts to obtain terminal degrees." Paul McStallworth cast Wesley's involvement in a more rigorous light:

> Individually and collectively, Wesley urged the faculty to obtain the doctorate degree. On other occasions he resorted to chiding them and warnings on the risk of loss of jobs without it, as indicated by Leonard Archer [who quotes him] in *Black Images in the American Theatre,* "Some of you are too lazy to drive fifty-five miles to Ohio State University." Most under his administration made some efforts to further their training and careers by study. Those who were successful in obtaining the degree usually received substantial increases in salary. Likewise promotion came with greater rapidity.

True to his paternalistic role, Wesley stood firm, but adapted his methods to the individual faculty member, and maintained high faculty spirit by amply rewarding those who bettered themselves.

A final positive feature in the lives of the Central State faculty was the opportunity offered by the school for participation in decision making. The North Central Association *Guide* recommends that

> the institution of higher education make every effort to promote a spirit of cooperation in which all the forces within the institution unite in the accomplishment of a common educational purpose. Policies and procedures should reflect the mutual support of the faculty and administrative officers for the institution's educational programs and activities.

In Kidd's extensive interviews with the 1958 faculty, they "generally expressed no adverse concern about their opportunity to participate in the academic administration of the College." He observed that "There was a feeling among them generally that they had an integral part in establishing and revising policies and procedures affecting the instructional program." Although this would seem to contradict the need for greater authority that President Groves discovered in the faculty in the mid 1960s, practices pertaining to faculty legislative authority appeared to be satisfactory during the Wesley years, both to the faculty members themselves and in relationship to the models with which Kidd compared them. Two faculty members concur that Wesley created an environment conducive to faculty input. Wilhelmina Robinson, former professor of history and chairman of the history department, admitted that Wesley "was very paternalistic, but he encouraged the faculty to come up with ideas and most of the time these ideas were implemented by his administration."[24] Former President Jackson cites several examples of faculty-administration cooperation and then concludes "President Wesley was always thinking of improvements in the academic program and after discussion, then with further consideration by faculty members in regular faculty meetings, new procedures were adopted."

In a further observation, Jackson aptly summarizes the positive nature of academic interaction within the Central State family during the Wesley years: "The school operated with a spirit of happiness, good will and serious educational intent. I felt that faculty relationships were pleasant and that most felt a spirit of steady improvement."

Those undeniable problems that did arise were generally attributed to outside factors, and the warmth and camaraderie between the faculty and other groups at the school continued.

One other interesting fact which supports the assertion that the college operated on principles very much like those of a family is the stability of the faculty. A survey of the April 1948 Bulletin of the College of Education and Industrial Arts (prior to its renaming) reveals a list of 113 faculty members. Of these persons, 25, or 22 percent, were still serving Central State University in 1965; some remain at the school even today.[25] Furthermore, of the 25 remaining through this period, 10 had attained advanced degrees (5 others already possessed the terminal degree in 1948). Nor were faculty members the only persons connected with the school who showed such long-term loyalty. The late Wilbur A. Page is another case in point. In November 1955, Dr. Page was honored by the college for his twenty-five years of faithful service on its Board of Trustees. Not only had he remained as a standard of continuity through the turmoil of the church-state split, but he had continuously supported the school and its individual students with gifts ranging from a pulpit Bible and an American platform flag to scholarship money. Three years earlier, the school had commended him through the presentation of an honorary degree, a Doctor of Divinity.[26]

Although there are only a handful of "Centralians" whose histories of service are as outstanding as that of Wilbur Page, stability, loyalty, interdependability, and cooperation were the hallmarks of the institution. This spirit could occasionally manifest itself in fierce ways, as, for example, on the eve of the church-state split. In Joseph Lewis's interview with Mildred Henderson, she describes it this way:

> Commencement was always on a Thursday, and you can imagine what happened when the word [of Wesley's dismissal] spread to the students. . . . That night we heard a lot of noise—the graduating class had torches and were marching down to Bishop Ransom's house. . . . The students were marching and singing: they said "come out wherever you are." Bishop Ransom was up in his room overlooking the situation. The students made an effigy and hung it up in his tree. . . . Students told him there would be no Commencement. . . . The students were very brave because we did not defy authority back in those days, especially the bishops'.

Not only does this incident seem striking in its boldness for 1948, but it illustrates to what extent students' loyalties were clearly attached not only to the inanimate entity, but to the man at its head. For them, the functions of the college were firmly rooted in its chief administrator—a situation much different than one would expect at a larger, less intimate school.

A final criterion suggested by the North Central Association for evaluating the programs of colleges and universities is an examination of student achievement. This section of their guidebook opens with the following caveat:

> Realistic expectations regarding the achievement of students must take into account the kinds and level of ability of students admitted to the institution. Grades in high school, rank in class, results of standardized aptitude and achievement tests, recommendations of high school personnel and others, and evidences of special interest and abilities.

By these standard measures, the entry-level abilities of many students who came to the college were not high. As Dr. Leonora C. Lane, who spent more than half a century in various faculty positions at the college, puts it, "We suffer a great many students here and we hope they will fall in line and graduate with some kind of prestige."[27] Indeed, the school recognized as part of its mission the acceptance of students who, because of past educational disadvantages, would doubtless have been rejected by other colleges—even public ones. In this regard, Central State may be viewed as a pioneer of the open admissions policy which later was legislatively mandated for all public colleges and universities in Ohio.

Lenient admissions standards were not, however, indicative of a similar attitude toward scholarship among students already enrolled. With the aid of the school's extensive remedial services, all students were expected eventually to attain a satisfactory level of college performance. During the 1950s, two safeguards—the sophomore comprehensive examinations and the senior comprehensive evaluations—were instituted to ensure that this would occur. These were later dropped but have recently been reinstated.

The 1951–52 Central State College Bulletin describes the sophomore comprehensive tests as follows:

> Sophomore comprehensive examinations will be given for all students, with classification below Junior, after 75 hours of college work have been completed, to determine their fitness to pursue studies on the upper level of the college and to determine how well they have achieved the following objectives:
>
> 1. The ability to read and use the English language accurately with reasonable facility and comprehension.
> 2. The ability to use simple mathematical calculations.
> 3. The ability for problem-solving according to basic principles of modern science.
> 4. The ability to display an intelligent attitude towards the social world.

131

5. The ability to read reasonably well one foreign, modern language.
Students who fail the examinations will be required to take them over, after having done remedial work.

Several interesting points arise in this description. First, it is clear from the scope of the tests that the liberal arts goal of the college was being maintained; a student could not proceed simply on the basis of talent in one area of study even though he might have been admitted on that basis. Second, the dedication of the school to real scholarship rather than the superficial accumulation of credits is evidenced in the fact that students were required to complete remedial work instead of simply retaking the examinations. And last, item four indicates the school's interest in nonintellectual variables by testing the students' attitudes to the world around them. Here again, the North Central Association's guidelines support the legitimacy of emphasis on such nonintellectual variables as attitudes, values, motivations, and personality traits in determining overall student achievement.

Similarly, the senior-level examinations included a "general culture examination" in addition to tests in the student's major field and professional tests for those receiving teaching certificates. Further, no course credit might be awarded for performance on these tests, so they could be considered a more objective proof of the student's knowledge than examinations in any individual course.

In the 1976–77 academic year, under the Newsom administration, a new competency-based English program was implemented in an attempt to regain these high ideals of academic performance. Homer Sippio, director of the academic foundations program, explained that a grade of "P" for "in progress" would henceforth replace the grades "D" and "F" for the required freshman English series, and in addition to regular classroom work, freshmen would take part in special assignments as required in the Reading Laboratory. Instructors were directed to set aside more individual tutoring time as well.

Essie K. Payne, associate professor of English who was named coordinator of the competency-based English component, spoke to the Alumni Association about the program:

> The students who continue in a course are given "growth time," and are better able to learn at their own rate. Even though the students could advance to the "C" level early in the following quarter, they are encouraged to stay on in the course to work toward more improvement and perhaps earn an even higher

grade. . . . The competency-based program also has a positive effect on subsequent courses.[28]

The ultimate proof, however, of a college's success in aiding its students to reach desired goals must always be in the student's performance after graduation. The North Central Association recommends: "Data on number and performance of graduates who continue in graduate or professional school is a useful measure of student achievement. . . . Follow-up studies of alumni . . . may provide data useful for evaluation purposes." Fortunately, Central State, in keeping with its tradition of strong personal ties among alumni and between alumni and the college, has kept records pertinent to this type of evaluation. A look at Table 2, provided by Walter Sellers, director of Office of University Relations and Alumni Affairs, shows Central State to be well represented by alumni who go on to achieve advanced degrees. For the period from 1950 to 1986, nearly 9 percent of Central State's 10,405 graduates went on to earn advanced degrees—954 attaining master's degrees and 204 attaining doctorate degrees (including M.D.'s and Juris Doctorates). These figures do not include the even larger number of students who may have pursued advanced study of a different nature of who may have taken graduate courses that did not result in a degree.

A far more informative and more engaging record of alumni achievement is contained in the publication *Alumni Profiles,* the purpose of which is to recognize and commend alumni of outstanding achievement.[29] The following observations may be gleaned from these *Alumni Profiles.* First in the listing of each person's awards, one often finds information about other publications in which he or she has been recognized. Citations in *World's Who's Who in Science, Outstanding Educators in America, Who's Who Among Black Americans,* and *Who's Who in the Midwest,* for example, are scattered throughout these biographical sketches, indicating that their alma mater is not alone in recognizing the special achievements of these men and women.

Second, the strong liberal arts emphasis at Central State is reflected not only in the diversity of the careers which its alumni eventually pursued, but in the diversity within many individual careers. It is not uncommon among these pages to find a single person whose endeavors have reached, for example, into research, private sector business, government service, and education. Interestingly too, although Central State's history as a teacher's college has produced a preponderance of educators among its distinguished alumni, many in the hard sciences and business—fields often underrepresented among educated blacks—are present here also. One may speculate that the supportive social atmosphere of the school, conducive to the flowering of individual potential, opened the way for such "nontraditional" career choices among its graduates. Similarly, the school's social atmosphere may have fostered the leadership traits evinced by many of these illustrious former students. Most not only have "moved up the ladder" in their chosen fields, but in their organizational affiliations they are often executive officers or members of directive boards.

Not surprisingly, many of these outstanding persons have combined their primary occupation with additional salaried or volunteer work in

TABLE 2
Total Number of Graduates for the Years 1950–1986

Year	Number of Graduates	Total Number of Advanced Degrees	Graduate Degrees	Doctorate
1950	216	35	31	4
1951	119	35	31	4
1952	111	16	14	2
1953	148	27	23	4
1954	136	40	33	7
1955	91	27	23	4
1956	179	44	38	6
1957	160	48	39	9
1958	172	47	38	9
1959	161	48	37	11
1960	166	40	31	9
1961	190	49	41	8
1962	147	60	49	11
1963	241	49	35	14
1964	310	66	51	15
1965	409	76	66	10
1966	278	47	37	10
1967	369	34	26	8
1968	367	54	44	10
1969	464	76	60	16
1970	513	60	48	12
1971	518	42	37	5
1972	481	37	31	6
1973	478	23	21	2

TABLE 2—*Continued*

Year	Number of Graduates	Total Number of Advanced Degrees	Graduate Degrees	Doctorate
1974	422	16	14	2
1975	380	15	11	4
1976	321	17	16	1
1977	284	6	6	0
1978	297	6	5	1
1979	290	7	7	0
1980	257	3	3	0
1981	287	5	5	0
1982	326	3	3	0
1983	259	0	0	0
1984	271	0	0	0
1985	312	0	0	0
1986	275	0	0	0
TOTAL	10,405	1,158	954*	204**

*Of the 1,158 graduates who have advanced degrees, 954 have a master's degree.
**Of the 1,158 graduates who have advanced degrees, 204 have a doctorate degree.

SOURCE: Chart obtained from the records of Walter G. Sellers, Central State University, Office of University Relations and Alumni Affairs, January 5, 1987.

"people-oriented" jobs. Teaching, at various educational levels, is frequently an adjunct to their research, administrative, performing, or counseling endeavors. Many have given service to their country, to their community, or to some special disadvantaged group—among these, women, the handicapped, veterans, the aged, youth, native Americans and, of course, blacks. Most have fought against discrimination either by personally breaking various color barriers or by researching and publishing the situation of black people in American society and assisting others—particularly young people—to escape the bonds of racism.

Finally, in addition to the interest they exhibit in education and in youth in general, many of these distinguished alumni have devoted particular time and effort to projects that benefit their alma mater. While much of this alumni support for the school must surely be attributed to individual generosity and concern, the network of local chapters and the central core, the General Alumni Association, did not just develop spontaneously. In this, too, the hand of long-time president Charles Wesley may be seen. Walter Sellers reports that from 1950 (before which no alumni association existed) until Wesley's retirement, no requests for donations were made, but at Wesley's urging, former graduates were encouraged to found strong local chapters involving as many persons as possible. Wesley himself maintained personal contact with many graduates for nearly twenty years after his retirement. By this method, an alumni network was built which has, since 1965, contributed thousands of dollars and many hours of time to worthwhile projects at the university—most notably the rebuilding and endowment efforts spearheaded by President Newsom. It has also encouraged scores of young people to choose a Central State education.

It is appropriate here, too, to recognize and praise the untiring work of Sellers himself. His efforts as an alumnus since 1951, and as director of university relations and alumni affairs since 1966, have made him an outstanding contributor not just to the health and growth of the CSU family, but to the larger community of Greene County. Indeed, it might be argued that Seller's work for other causes—the establishment of the Greene County Vocational School, the Central State-Xenia Appreciation Day, and post-tornado assistance for the Xenia School District (for which he was a long-time Board of Education member)—has brought favorable recognition to the university just as valuable as his direct service to it.[30]

Yet a last manifestation of alumni support not mentioned in the criteria of the North Central Association is the tendency of alumni to send their children to their former school. A high number of subsequent-generation students is both an indication of the success of the institution and of the satisfaction felt by its alumni. First, to encourage one's children to attend college at all requires a conviction about the value of a college education—a conviction which is not likely to exist unless one's own college work contributed to the attainment of various career and life goals. And additionally, one must have a feeling that the particular college experience at one's own former school was the best of its kind available. Without a doubt, many Central State University alumni have these feelings about their alma mater.

While alumni associations are ubiquitous at both public and private colleges and universities throughout the country, an outstanding auxiliary organization has also been functioning on behalf of Central State for four decades. It is the National Association of Central State University Mothers. In addition to the substantial fund-raising and recruitment projects they have undertaken throughout the years, the University Mothers have supported high scholastic goals by recognizing "Outstanding Students" for their academic achievements, and at one time they had fostered greater appreciation of the staff—an often neglected group in university hierarchies—through their "Mother of the Year" award.

Walter Sellers has stated that approximately 50 percent of today's students at Central State have close relatives who have attended in the past.[31] Obviously there are many persons who strive to make members of their family members of the Central State family as well.

seven

A Commitment
to Excellence

Dr. Arthur E. Thomas became, on January 28, 1985, the first of Central State's presidents to be elected from among the ranks of its alumni. Thomas is a person of strong internal contrasts. Although he is remembered as a 1960s Civil Rights activist who for several years directed a student rights center, he has taken a firm stand in dealing with student discipline.

He has dedicated himself to enhancing the scholarly prestige of his qualified faculty and rewarding their efforts with "the highest possible salaries." Unlike his predecessor, who he feels "believed that professors and staff members of Central State University should sacrifice salary to keep the University open," Thomas thinks people "should be paid their market value." Although he would never state it so crudely, one infers readily from Thomas's words that those whose "market value" is low ought to beware.[1] Among his tasks will be to achieve fiscal solvency in an era of declining federal dollars, both in direct aid and student support; to upgrade the high tech capabilities of both staff and students and to forge the best university business alliances within an increasingly competitive and uncertain labor market; and to carve out a more specialized niche of expertise in the larger community of higher education. All this, of course, he and his successors will be expected to accomplish while walking the historic tightrope of the traditionally black institution—the fine balances between maintaining and expanding academic excellence and providing a safety net for the academically disadvantaged, between opening the doors to more nonblack students and staff and sustaining a nurturing environment for the black cultural experience.

Balancing the Central State University budget is not an impossible task—a fact readily apparent in the strides already made by the new administration. The October 24, 1985 issue of *The Gold Torch* proudly proclaimed, "CSU Finance Brightens Up," due in large measure to the $2 million supplement to its usual biennial appropriation from the Ohio General Assembly. Also on the plus side was increased enrollment—an all-time high of 2,680 in September 1985. And CSU had achieved nearly one-third of the $1 million goal for alumni endowment.

In part, this "new money" has been pledged through traditional fund-raising methods, but three very innovative plans are being tried as well. The first draws upon the typical alumni fondness for the home school's sports teams. The Central State Marauder Scholarship Foundation encourages former students to help future ones through scholarships, grants, and other types of financial aid. A second avenue for giving allows alumni to aid the university while protecting their families with life insurance. Explained by Walter Sellers in the December 1985 issue of the *Alumni Journal,* this plan uses part of the contributor's premium to pay for the insurance, while the remainder is placed in a separate "Premium Deposit Fund" where it draws interest for the university. If only 100 persons take part at the minimum monthly premium of $50 per month, the school will have received $210,000 by 1990. Finally, the most unusual of these creative new plans was the Alumni Association's contract with Cernitin America, Inc., a multi-level marketing organization spearheaded at that time by Dr. David Allen, a 1969 CSU graduate. As with the insurance plan, a percentage system allows alumni-distributors to increase their own incomes marketing Cernitin's vitamins and food supplements while building Central State's endowment as well.[2]

Certainly, no university in the era of Graham-Rudman, the dismantling of the U.S. Department of Education, and the demographic decline of 18- to 24-year-olds can afford to become complacent about funding. It should be noted, too, that the achievement of financial solvency was not without discomfort among students or staff. Replacement of the student college cash program with a greater emphasis on college work study has proven an effective but not altogether popular measure.[3] At the advice of Touche-Ross and Company, an independent accounting firm hired to help straighten out the university's financial predicament, Thomas informed the trustees that he was asking the Ohio attorney general to prosecute approximate 2,000 former students with unpaid debts. According to Richard M. Norman, vice-president for finance and administration, some $3 million is owed by persons who have dropped out or graduated over

DR. ARTHUR E. THOMAS
VICE-PRESIDENT FOR
ACADEMIC AFFAIRS (1977)
PRESIDENT (1985)
ALUMNUS OF CSU
CLASS OF 1962

the past twenty-four years. But until collections become a reality, many austerity measures will remain in place.[4] Indeed, Thomas himself began his tenure as president at a salary somewhat lower than that of his predecessor. Belt tightening is often paired with the rolling up of sleeves as well, and here, too, the new president sets a vigorous example. The June 15, 1986 issue of *The Gold Torch* included a snapshot of President Thomas and Dean Jackson joining faculty and students for a campus cleanup day coordinated by Audrey Norman-Turner, associate dean of students.[5]

There is also a determination that Central State should enter its second century better prepared for the technology of the future. Under the guidance of Dr. Thyrsa Svager, vice-president for academic affairs, computer literacy has gained importance as a freshman requirement. A Level II computer literacy thrust will provide more in-depth integration of computer applications to students' individual areas of study. This is but the first of many enhancements intended to ready Central State to meet the technological demands of the twenty-first century. The Ohio Board of Regents has given approval for a four-year Bachelor of Science degree in manufacturing engineering. Dr. William Grissom, who chairs the department, explains that now is an ideal time for such a program because "manufacturing industries are undergoing revolutionary changes which are creating a demand for more sophisticated manufacturing education."[6] Central's proximity to Dayton, Cincinnati, and Columbus is another important factor.

To utilize the university's nearness to the Air Force Logistics Command at Wright Patterson Air Force Base, a research committee proposed in early 1986 the development of a logistics option within the existing Bachelor of Science in business administration and later a full-fledged degree program in logistics management. Similarly, in May 1986, the university announced the receipt of $100,000 in state and federal grants for robotics research. Carl White, CSU research associate, approached the National Aeronautics and Space Administration about its use of the robotic arm that will be developed on NASA's planned space station.

Two high-demand allied health fields—physical therapy and health care administration—constitute equally attractive new programs for Central State. In physical therapy especially, minorities are currently underrepresented, so this program should yield many employment opportunities for graduates. Similarly, a proposed degree program in fashion merchandising technology will help satisfy the shortage of qualified personnel in today's complex and sophisticated consumer market. Nor is Central State neglecting the academic area that has long been its forte—teacher training. It is committed to establishing, before 1992

> an endowed chair to attract nationally acclaimed professors in the field of education. With this endowed chair, the College of Education will work with private and public organizations to research and develop an innovative curriculum that can be used to teach, in systematic manner, the principles and philosophy of the holistic approach to urban education.[8]

Although the emphasis in all of these plans is on programming and personnel, concurrent improvements in the physical plant and university equipment are taking place. One such improvement has come about as a result of $90,000 equipment grant from AT&T for microcomputers and a major overhaul of the university's mainframe capacity to benefit mathematics and computer science majors. This latter project especially reflects the financial realities of the 1980s as well. The new VAX 11/780 system "was financed with a $157,000 grant from Title III, a $155,000 grant from the Ohio Board of Regents, and $11,425 from the Digital Corporation."[9]

Similarly, institution of improved honors programs and proficiency testing procedures have attempted to address the technological demands of the future. Ever since the 1979 accreditation evaluation, Central State had been aware of the need for more accurate and comprehensive testing procedures. The system that has been instituted assesses incoming freshmen to determine which of three foundations programs will be most beneficial to them. Another phase of the program will chart students' progress through their undergraduate years, and a final phase will prepare them with specialized testing skills needed to achieve high scores on standard admission tests for graduate and professional schools.

Clearly, the keystone of the testing program is the ability to individualize curricula for freshmen. The Honors Program and its associated President's Scholarships and Page Hall Honors Dormitory are designed to attract and hold an elite corps of students whose high academic achievement will set performance standards for the entire student body as well as boost the morale and sharpen the competitive edge of faculty members. The University College will assist incoming students who are not yet prepared for college-level work, while average students will continue to be served in the established freshman program.

An element crucial to the success of the new University College has begun to receive national acclaim as well. A January 8, 1986 article in

142

Education Week highlighted the work of the ad hoc Select Committee on the Education of Black Youth organized by Thomas and chaired by Dr. Alvin Poussaint of Harvard University Medical School. The committee has endorsed "Foundations for Learning: Language," the experimental curriculum in use in Central State's University College. The curriculum "abandons remediation as the road to standard English in favor of methods that encourage learning through self-expression." "Foundations for Learning" has been test-marketed in high schools as well, and preliminary data show that it has the potential to improve students' scores by as much as 27 percent in a single academic year.[10]

One question raised by James Crawford, interviewer for *Education Week,* regarding the "Foundations for Learning" curriculum is how it relates to the issue of changing the dialect spoken by many urban black students. To this Thomas replies, "Granted the English language itself has racist aspects—but if black youth can't negotiate standard English, they can't negotiate the world of employment."[11]

This toughminded, pragmatic approach is united with a commitment to maintaining traditional ties with black students' African heritage. In the spring of 1986, Thomas participated in a tour of development programs sponsored by Operation Crossroads Africa, the thirty-year-old program upon which the U.S. Peace Corps was modeled. While abroad, he discussed potential cooperative projects with various government and university officials. Acting on one plan to make Central State's African students feel more "at home," he and Mrs. Thomas hosted a costumed "International Friendship Affair" featuring food and entertainment from the over twenty countries represented on the campus.[12]

The possibility of Central's contributing to greater black representation in the State Department's Foreign Service has also been pondered. More extensive preparation in French, the official language in several African and Caribbean nations, and the improvement of student test-taking skills have been cited as two means of preparing students for this highly selective occupation.

Although traditional avenues for black college graduates have been heavily skewed in favor of education and social and governmental service, economic realities now demand a greater bond between Central State and the industrial and commercial entities to which its students must increasingly look for employment. This change, too, is not without discomfort. Jim Hardin, former associate director of the cooperative education department complains, "The problem with the average student is that they are so eager to graduate that they fail to prepare for after graduation."[13]

143

Methods for increasing student capacity to accept sacrifice and delayed rewards and to confront the rigors of the business community must be found.

Recent strides to produce linkages to the business community have been impressive, both in terms of the exchange of knowledge and in vastly improved public relations. Laurence S. Newman, Jr., associate editor of the Dayton *Journal Herald,* praised Thomas's appointment of a sixteen-member President's Council. Newman quoted member Joshua Smith, president and chief executive officer of MAXIMA Corp., a high-tech support firm that ranks among the nation's top 100 black-owned businesses. According to Smith,

> We advise him [Thomas] as CEOs . . . about good programs and marketing those programs. . . . We serve as a resource, quarterly, sharing how we work as companies. . . .
> When we say we're setting a priority, we do it. . . . Before we leave a meeting, we decide we're going to see some program . . . , something measurable. . . . We set dates, absolute deadlines.

So enamored of corporate models and methods of achieving excellence has Thomas become that his first Special Presidential Report, "A Commitment to Excellence" was prefaced by quotations from *In Search of Excellence: Lessons from America's Best Run Companies,* by Thomas J. Peters and Robert H. Waterman, Jr., and *Iacocca: An Autobiography,* by Lee Iacocca. Special attention has been given to corporate and foundation gifts established to assure that not only advice but dollars would be forthcoming from these improved corporate-university ties. The benefits are not, however, intended to flow solely in the direction of the university. An Institute for Minority Business was proposed to increase CSU's public service activities in support of minority business people.

Although many of Central State's plans are geared toward national or even international recognition, steps have been taken to improve town-gown relationships in the local community as well. One special program allows pre-law students to obtain insights about their future career by observing and helping in Xenia law offices. On a broader scale, the university initiated regular meetings with Greene County law enforcement agencies to improve relations. Xenia police chief Dan Aultman has said that these meetings have allowed agencies to separate "perceived problems" from real ones. Similarly, Mark Short, 1985–87 Student Government Association president, launched talks with the Xenia Area Chamber of Commerce to address topics of concern to merchants—such as increased levels of shoplifting during school sessions—and of concern to Central students—such as increased opportunities for employment.[14]

While individual students need to broaden their education, Central State is today faced with the seemingly contradictory challenge of choosing areas of specialization in which it can excel. On a personal level, Thomas and his wife, Betty Dungy Thomas, initiated an innovative fine arts concept to showcase Ohio's African-American artists. The year-long exhibit, which precedes the anticipated opening of the Afro-American Museum adjacent to the university, is unique not only in its collection of art works, but in the fact that they are arrayed throughout the presidential home. At the end of the year, several of the works will be selected for purchase by the university for its permanent collection.[15]

Perhaps the most outstanding example of this search for uniqueness may be found in its establishment of the International Center for Water Resources Development. According to the university's brochure, the center will

—provide undergraduate education in the social, political, economic, and technical aspects of water resources management.

—provide continuing education to water resources technicians in the social, political, and economic issues of water resources management.

—provide continuing education to political leaders in the technical aspects of water resources management.

—provide extension services in water resources management to Ohio and to developing countries throughout the world, through the extension arm of The Ohio State University.

—conduct research in effective water management strategies and technologies.

—attract minorities into water resources management careers.

To publicize its anticipated September 1987 opening, the center held a Water Day Festival on May 14, 1986, which included preliminary exhibits on programs and careers, speeches by local officials, music by local groups, and performances by The Ohio State University Synchronized Swim Team. The center has the unique advantage of allowing Central State to become a leader in the critical issue of water supply and management both for Ohio and in the larger context of Third World planning. Through this project, Central State will have an opportunity to forge alliances in the international community of higher education—typified by its cooperative agreement with the state of Israel and Febbraio '74 of

Rome, Italy. At the same time, it will have an opportunity to provide humanitarian service on an international scale.

The International Center for Water Resources Development also illustrates a fresh approach to bridging the historic gap between serving the special interests of the black community and preparing students for success in a multi-cultural, predominantly white society. One of the center's first projects, for example, is scheduled to be an inventory of water supply and water management activities in drought-plagued Africa, and it is expected to attract and place many minority students as its work progresses. At the same time, water conservation issues are among the most universal concerns in Ohio and the rest of the United States. If such cooperation can be achieved on an international scale, what does the future hold for Central State's relationship with other Ohio schools?

From early signs, the future bodes well for Central State's linkages among Ohio's public colleges and universities. In the water resources project, the school has allied itself closely with The Ohio State University, credited in its brochure as "one of the nation's largest and most advanced land grant universities with extensive international water resources experiences." Central State has also taken to heart the advice of Dr. Manning Marable of Colgate University, whose column, "Along the Color Line," is syndicated in more than 140 newspapers. Marable stated in a 1985 article:

> Black colleges must establish structural ties with two-year institutions to ensure that black students make the transition to complete their B.A. degree. . . . Yet there is also the related tendency . . . to attempt to provide too many programs with too few resources. . . . Many Black colleges have been too reluctant . . . to focus on several specific academic fields, while cross-listing courses at neighboring universities which have resources or faculty in other areas.[16]

While the traditional relationship among institutions of higher education has been one of competition rather than cooperation, the future demands that curricular duplication be eliminated and transfer of credits be standardized. Similarly, faculty who in the past jealously guarded their academic turf and fought whenever possible to maintain it must now be re-educated to see the benefits of consolidation. How will Thomas deal with these challenges? If his first eighteen months in office is an accurate yardstick, Thomas's handling of this and other thorny problems will be efficient and effective. Cooperative agreements have already been hammered out between Central State and Cuyahoga Community and Sinclair

Community colleges with the help of Governor Richard Celeste and the Ohio Board of Regents. Some articulation documents, such as transfer guides, were completed in time for the beginning of the 1986–87 academic year, and the first of the Cuyahoga Community College graduates have begun to register.

Two of the keys to Thomas's ability to accomplish what other, equally dedicated men have not, are his youthful vigor and enthusiasm and his diplomatic, team-centered approach. He has been aptly labeled a "firebrand," a man "concerned about his weaknesses," and a "catalyst." He misses no opportunity to thank publicly those who have aided him or his beloved Central State. Notably, trustees, Ohio legislators and executive officials, federal agency representatives, evaluating committee members, as well as the media (who were in the past often criticized for helping Central State too little) are now praised for their assistance. Likewise, faculty, fellow administrators, and students may be admonished in private, but it is their positive contributions that are made public.

In addition to being a team player, Thomas has an admirable talent for surrounding himself with a stellar "team." No lesser national celebrities than Jesse Jackson and Bill Cosby aligned themselves with Central State during Thomas's first year-and-a-half in office. Jackson spoke at the Charter Day Convocation to announce the establishment of the Jesse L. Jackson PUSH/EXCEL Chair in the College of Education, dedicated to developing research strategies to institutionalize PUSH/EXCEL concepts in schools nationwide. Cosby accepted an honorary doctorate and established a $100,000 scholarship fund in honor of his friend, the late John Bowser, former executive director of the Philadelphia Urban Coalition. He even mentioned Central State as a quality university within the dialogue of his acclaimed *The Cosby Show*—a "mention" heard by millions of viewers.[17] This is a chapter of Central State history which is yet unwritten. One thing, however, is clear: an institution that survives the trial by fire of the late 1980s will emerge stronger than ever.

Appendix A

Honorary Degrees Conferred by Central State University 1951–1986

LL.D. – Doctor of Laws
D.D. – Doctor of Divinity
D.SC. – Doctor of Science
L.H.D. – Doctor of Humane Letters

YEAR	NAME	HONORARY DEGREE
1951	Sen. Albert L. Daniels	LL.D.
	Dr. Harry E. Davis	LL.D.
1952	Dr. Ray E. Hughes	LL.D.
	Dr. Bland L. Stradley	LL.D.
1953	Dr. Walter White	LL.D.
	Mr. Ladislas Segy	L.H.D.
1954	Mr. John H. Johnson	LL.D.
	Dr. M. C. Clarke	LL.D.
	Dr. Joseph H. Jackson	D.D.
	Dr. J. Welby Broaddus	D.D.
1955	Dr. William L. Monahan	LL.D.
	Rev. Wilbur A. Page	D.D.
	Dr. Charles H. Mahoney	LL.D.
1956	Dr. Charles S. Johnson	LL.D.
	Dr. James C. Evans	LL.D.
	Dr. Stella Counselbaum	L.H.D.
	Dr. Walter E. Kutch	D.D.

YEAR	*NAME*	*HONORARY DEGREE*
1957	Dr. Braxton F. Cann	D.Sc.
	Dr. J. Clayton Ettinger	LL.D.
	Dr. J. Arnett Mitchell	L.H.D.
	Dr. Louis H. Rawls	D.D.
	Mr. Jay William Holmes	L.H.D.
1958	Rabbi SeTwyn Ruslander	D.D.
	Judge Roscoe Walcutt	LL.D.
	Todd Duncan	D.Mus.
	Martin Luther King, Jr.	L.H.D.
1959	Dr. Truman Gibson, Sr.	D.B.A.
	Dr. George W. Lucas	D.D.
	Dr. Harold L. Yochum	L.H.D.
1960	J. Maynard Dickerson	LL.D.
	James H. N. Waring, Jr.	L.H.D.
	Stephen M. Young	LL.D.
	Dr. Carl J. Murphy	LITT.D.
	Mr. William B. Saxbe	LL.D.
1961	Dr. James T. Jeremiah '60	D.D.
	Dr. John G. Lewis	L.H.D.
	Attorney Charles C. Diggs	LL.D.
	Dr. Paul Katz	D.Mus.
	Dr. Clifford C. Davis	D.Sc.
1962	Mr. Roy Wilkins	LL.D.
	Dr. Charles J. Carney	L.H.D.
	Dr. Peter Marshall Murray	D.Sc.
1963	Mr. Berl I. Bernhard	LL.D.
	Rev. H. Beecher Hicks	D.D.
	Mr. Kivie Kaplan	L.H.D.
1964	Mr. Arthur Beerman	L.H.D.
	Dr. Novice Fawcett	LL.D.
	Mr. Charles Garvin	D.Sc.
1965	Atty. Jack Greenberg	LL.D.
	Judge Augustus Parker	LL.D.
	Mr. J. Walter Willis	D.H.
	Dr. Paul W. Briggs	Ed.D.
	Mr. James Griffin	LL.D.
	Mr. John W. Davis	LL.D.

Appendix A

YEAR	NAME	HONORARY DEGREE
1966	Dr. Gerald Acker	D.Sc.
	Dr. Edward Irons '48	LL.D.
	Sen. Charles Whalen, Jr.	LL.D.
	Mr. Glenn A. Rich	LL.D.
	Dr. William Young	LL.D.
1967	Dr. Nathan Christopher	LL.D.
	Dr. Kenneth W. Clement	LL.D.
	Cong. Michael Kirwan	LL.D.
	Mr. Carl B. Stokes	LL.D.
	Mr. William O. Walker	LL.D.
1968	Atty. Charles Carr	LL.D.
	Dr. Murrill Szucs	D.Sc.
	Dr. John Millett	LL.D.
	Mr. Robert C. Henry	LL.D.
	Mr. James D. Fain	LL.D.
	Miss Leontyne Price	D. Music
1969	Rev. L. Venchael Booth	L.H.D.
	Atty. W. Howard Fort	LL.D.
	Atty. Harvey Johnson	LL.D.
1970	Rev. Leon Sullivan	LL.D.
	Atty. John Bustamente	LL.D.
	Mr. C. Jaxon Dale	LL.D.
1971	Mr. James E. Farmer '67	LL.D.
	Mayor James H. McGee	LL.D.
1972	Asst. Secy. Samuel Jackson	LL.D.
	Rep. William Mallory '55	LL.D.
	Atty. Edward J. Cox	LL.D.
	Atty. Lawrence Curtis	LL.D.
	Mr. Lowell Schleicher	LL.D.
1973	Judge Robert M. Duncan	LL.D.
	Dr. Benjamin L. Hooks	L.H.D.
	Mr. Kenneth C. Ray	L.H.D.
	Mr. John J. Gilligan	LL.D.
1974	Dr. Barbara Sizemore	LL.D.
	Dr. O'Neil D. Swanson	D.Sc.
	Mr. Lloyd E. Lewis	LL.D.
1975	Dr. Effie O. Ellis	D.Sc.
	Mr. Samuel G. Sava	LL.D.

150

YEAR	*NAME*	*HONORARY DEGREE*
1976	Mr. C. J. McLin, Jr.	LL.D.
	Mrs. Bernice Sumlin	LL.D.
	Mr. Carl S. Jenkins	D.Sc.
	Mr. Phillip R. Shriver	LL.D.
	Mrs. Nancy Wilson Burton	D.Mu.
1977	Mr. Joe Black	LL.D.
	Dr. Rembert Stokes	LL.D.
	Dr. Robert Kegerreis	LL.D.
	Dr. Dwight Pemberton	D.Sc.
1978	Mr. Richard Johnson	D.Sc.
	Mr. James S. Wade	LL.D.
1979	Mrs. Rosa Parks	LL.D.
	Ms. Maya Angelou	LL.D.
	Mr. Arnold Pinkney	LL.D.
1980	Rep. Damon J. Keith	LL.D.
	Dr. William DuPree	LL.D.
	Mr. Dennis Dowdell, Jr.	LL.D.
1981	Ms. Charlotte Glueck	LL.D.
	Dr. Harold L. Enarson	LL.D.
	Mr. Charles Moody, Sr.	LL.D.
1982	Ms. Anne Pruitt	LL.D.
	Mr. William F. Bowen	LL.D.
	Mr. Carl O. Arehart	D. Pedagogy
1983	Mr. Arthur Jefferson	LL.D.
	Mr. Frank Foster	D. Music
1984	Dr. Edmund Casey	LL.D.
	Sen. M. Morris Jackson	LL.D.
	Dr. Lionel H. Newsom	D. Music
	Mr. William "Count" Basie	LL.D.
	Mrs. Catherine Basie	LL.D.
1985	Mr. Louis Stokes	LL.D.
	Dr. Theodore Johnson	LL.D.
	Rep. Michael DeWine	LL.D.
	Mr. Robert Lamb, Jr.	LL.D.
	Mr. Gerald E. Dackin	L.H.D.
1986	Judge Lloyd O. Brown	LL.D.
	Mr. William G. Sykes	LL.D.
	Dr. John E. Jacob	LL.D.

Appendix B

Board of Trustees

153

Appendix C

Central State University Alumnus of the Year Award

1970
BERNARD GREGORY
'48
CHICAGO, ILLINOIS

1972
WALTER SELLERS
'51
WILBERFORCE, OHIO

1973
JAY CROSBY
'50
DAYTON, OHIO

1975
JAMES FARMER
'67
DAYTON, OHIO

1979
JUNE MARABLE
'48
DAYTON, OHIO

1980
ORLANDO BAYLOR
'49
WASHINGTON, DC

1982
MAURICE REED
'50
SPRINGFIELD, OHIO

1983
TYREE BROOMFIELD
'73
DAYTON, OHIO

1976
ELLA DOSS
'52
CLEVELAND, OHIO

1977
ANN GATES
'46
AKRON, OHIO

1978
JANETTE HARRIS
'62
WASHINGTON, DC

1984
GLORIA TOWERS
'54
CLEVELAND, OHIO

1985
CONSTANCE HARPER
'54

1986
JOSHUA I. SMITH
'63

Appendix D

**Central State University
General Alumni Association Presidents**

1. MR. SAMUEL D. HOUSTON (1951–52)
2. MR. KENNETH TATE (1952–56)
3. ATTORNEY JAMES COBB (1956–58)
4. MR. BERNARD GREGORY (1958–60)
5. MRS. EDNA REESE BATTEE (1960–62)
6. MRS. MYRTLE KILLIBREW RUSH (1962–64)
7. MR. KENNETH BLACKBURN (1952–56)
8. THE HONORABLE GLENN T. JOHNSON (1966–68)
9. MRS. JEAN LANE PARKER (1968–70)
10. MRS. NANCY TRAVIS BOLDEN (1970–72)
11. MR. WILLIAM H. HARDY (1972–74)
12. MR. DENNIS DOWDELL, JR. (1975–78)
13. MR. JAMES E. FARMER (1979–82)
14. MRS. GLORIA TAYLOR TOWERS (1982–present)

Appendix E

Central State University Retirement Roster 1955–1986

YEAR RETIRED	NAME	DEPARTMENT	YEARS OF SERVICE
1955	Jean H. Walls	Psychology	7
1956	Haywood Willis	Maintenance	13
1957	Jimsiana Brassfield	Home Economics	27
	Beverly Heard	Math	10
1958	Delmer Bowen	Power Plant	9
	Dorothy Zeiger	Intercultural Ed.	10
1959	Inez Mercer	Clerk	39
1960	Maude Howard	Maintenance	11
1961	William W. Brown	Electrician	37
	Arthur Chavous	Math	37
	James Newsome	Education	37
	Ralph Pyrtle	Biology	14
	Herbert White	Cashier	11
1962	George Franklin David	Sociology	22
	Lillian Watts Foster	English	15
	Burton Turner	Watchman	7
1963	John B. Anderson	Power Plant	18
	Homer H. Collins	Maintenance	20
	Effie Lee Newsome	Library	11
1964	Elizabeth M. Anderson	Dean of Women	19
	James Day	Security	8
	Charles W. Hall	Attendent	3
	Alfred Leach	Engineer	15

Appendix E

YEAR RETIRED	NAME	DEPARTMENT	YEARS OF SERVICE
1965	Bertie M. Coleman	Library	8
	John Elery	Watchman	17
	Lottie D. Harrison	Industrial Arts	16
	Burt Means	Maintenance	14
	Stanley Rose	Maintenance	35
	Jesse V. Taylor	Maintenance	46
	Anna Terry	Music	31
1966	James Anderson	Carpentry	30
	Clarence A. Caliman	Library	48
	William R. Harris	Maintenance	19
	William L. Jones	Maintenance	40
	Isaac Sappe Lane	Biology	19
	Ramona Matson	Nursing	18
	Benjamin Mitchell	Maintenance	19
	Dorsey T. Murray	Business Admin.	29
	Clayburn Robinson	Engineer	14
	Josephine Smith	Housing	4
1967	Marcella Austin	Art	40
	Gladys Powell	Registrar	38
1968	Robert Herbertson	Accounting	3
	Thomas Dudley Howe	Biology	8
	Nellie J. Lewis	Maintenance	15
	Ralph Templin	Sociology	20
1969	Mary V. H. Fisher	Switchboard	20
	Abbott Rick	English	3
1970	Donald Leroy Simpson	Maintenance	21
1971	Wilbur M. Harper	Grounds	34
1972	Raymond Barnett	Carpenter	18
	Inez M. Boddy	Library	27
	Edna Lucille Carter	Maintenance	20
	Etta Vera Corbin	Cashier	12
	John Lang, Sr.	Cafeteria	14
	George Nooks	Cafeteria	15
	W. Lou Tandy	Economics	18
1973	Raymond Barnett	Maintenance	20
	Alfred Dawson	Maintenance	25
	Gaston F. Lewis	Athletics	26
	Fred Matson	Maintenance	9

YEAR RETIRED	NAME	DEPARTMENT	YEARS OF SERVICE
1973 (con't)	Oliver Mynatt	Receiving	17
	Ruth McCants	Business Office	26
	Thelma Turner	Business Education	26
	George F. Woodson, Jr.	Math	25
	E. Oscar Woolfolk	Chemistry	23
1974–75	William Carter	Maintenance-Library	15
	Lottie Cobbs	Bookstore	32
	Clarence Cordell	Maintenance	21
	Mary Fisher	Library	28
	James Harrison	Psychology	26
	Bernice Hughes	Foreign Language	12
	Arletta Johnson	Education	25
	Geraldine Johnson	Dormitory	9
	Mary E. Lee	Sociology	24
	Helen Means	Library	20
	Robert McKinney	Food Service	25
	Herman Robinson	Garage	29
	Wilhelmina Robinson	History	31
	Thelma Sullivan	Dormitory	13
	Arlesia West	Food Service	7
	Raymond West	Maintenance	26
	Anne Williamson	Editor	43
1976	Richard Burling	Physics	15
	John Lee Cole	Maintenance	9
	John H. Cooper	Biology	28
	William Cunningham	Grounds	33
	Louise S. Garcia	HPER	36
	Forrest Rhoden	Maintenance	6
	Jaroy Thomas	Power Plant	8
	Jason Turner, Sr.	Maintenance	11
	Sammye S. Walker	English	29
1977	Albert Baker	HPER	30
	Gertrude Engel	Foreign Language	29
	Henry A. Garcia	Music	26
	Nicolas Gerren	Learning Center	10
	Foster Harris	Grounds	24
	James T. Henry	Earth Sciences	29
	Hercules H. Hensley	Garage	20
	Elizabeth L. Jennings	Accounting (Payable)	13

Appendix E

YEAR RETIRED	NAME	DEPARTMENT	YEARS OF SERVICE
1977 (con't)	Harry G. Johns	Bus. Adm. (Acting Dean)	28
	Chaney L. Lucas	Dormitory Maintenance	16
	Ernestyne Williams	Food Service	14
	Mozetta Wright	Health Center	22
1978	Hayward R. Dinsmore	Art	28
	Rosa Emery	Food Service	31
	Frank Glenn	Maintenance	31
	Mildred B. Green	Library	31
	Essie K. Payne	English	28
	William P. Priser	Food Service	11
	Paul Richardson	Grounds	29
1979	Jennetta Cousin	Food Service	31
	Thomas J. Craft	Biology	29
	Cecil Davis	Cafeteria	15
	James E. Hamilton	Power Plant	28
	Stanley Kirton	Music (Dean)	24
	Alva Lucas	Maintenance	18
	Lovella Lucas	Maintenance	17
1980	Juanita Anderson	Switchboard	27
	Dorothy Chapman	Food Service (Director)	18
	Frances Hawkins	Registrar	31
	Leonard Jackson	Power Plant	27
	Fred Mabra	Dormitory	30
	Beatrice Moore	Dormitory	30
	Marjorie Swanson	Maintenance	21
	Helene Taylor	Physical Plant	19
1981	John Alston	Social Welfare	34
	Frances Thomas	Philosophy	34
	Gertrude Upton	Accounts Payable	6
1982	Ruth Bailey	Health Center (B.F. Lee)	11
	Gladys Confer	Alumni	12
	Wanetta Greer	Maintenance	13
	James Hartsfield	Maintenance	10
	Zenobia Perry	Music	26
	Doris Richardson	Library	23
	Ruth Stewart	Purchasing	30

YEAR RETIRED	NAME	DEPARTMENT	YEARS OF SERVICE
1983	Katherine Anderson	Maintenance	16
	Mildred Henderson	Secretarial Services	37
	Joy Mackay	Education	11
	Beatrice O'Rourke	Music	37
	Albert D. Pitts	Power Plant	22
	Nerissa Wray	Maintenance	32
1984	Bonnie Bowman	Food Service	29
	Eugene Brady	Maintenance	12
	Paul Calloway	Maintenance	17
	Warren Cordell	Maintenance	17
	Ahler Harris	Water	17
	Allen Rodgers	Security	23
	Paul White	Maintenance	13
1985	Joseph L. Anthony	Administration	5
	Allyson Barrett	Library	19
	Grace Ferris	Maintenance	27
	Jennie Glenn	Maintenance	36
	David Hazel	Admin. Dean	27
	Thelma J. Kelley	Accounting	27
	Mary Miner	Library	8
	Lionel Newsom	President	12
	Ella J. Turner	Maintenance	37
	Lucille Walls	Maintenance	13
	Thomas West	Grounds	22
1986	Margaret Adams	Alumni	18
	Mae Baker	Student Services	25
	Curtis Bowman	Security	31
	Charles Christopher	Receiving	19
	Beatrice Clark	Food Service	20
	Christine Edmondson	Dean College of Arts & Sciences	17
	George Harper	Maintenance	16
	Herman Honaker	Security	22
	Thomas E. Kelley, Sr.	Purchasing	40
	John McPherson	Power Plant	17
	Stanley Saunders	Food Service	32
	Virginia Stills	Food Service	33
	Jesse Taylor, Jr.	Power Plant	30
	Herbert Willis	Business Admin.	24

Notes

Sources of Data

Most of the data for this book were secured from the following primary sources: (1) annual reports of the president, (2) minutes of the Board of Trustees, (3) catalogs, bulletins, and school papers of Central State University, (4) reports of special faculty committees, (5) personal and institutional papers of Dr. Charles Wesley, from collections in the Moorland-Springarn Research Center, Manuscript Division, Washington, D.C.; the Hallie Q. Brown Library Archives, Central State University; the National Archives at Howard University; and Dr. Wesley's home in Washington, D.C., (6) oral interviews with Dr. Charles Wesley as well as interviews with alumni and citizens of the Wilberforce community, (7) Ohio Board of Regents, *Basis of Data Series: Ohio Higher Education System,* (8) class annuals, (9) reports of committees from accrediting agencies, (10) records in the various offices of the University, (11) addresses by Central State's president, (12) mimeographed bulletins in the various offices of the University, (13) descriptive accounts of the University by Charles H. Wesley and alumni, (14) addresses of Founder's Day speakers, and (15) correspondence with the deans and other individuals who have knowledge of the development of the institution. Data of a secondary nature were secured from (1) works on American higher education, (2) miscellaneous articles on black education, and (3) newspaper and magazine articles about Central State University.

Chapter 1

[1]Josephus R. Coan, *Daniel Payne: Christian Educator* (Philadelphia: AME Book Concern, 1935). Among Bishop Payne's rules for campus behavior were a proper observance of study hours, no use of tobacco or stimulants, no association between the sexes in any

form without permission, no visiting the kitchen, and no absence from the campus or visiting with families without permission. Chapel and Sunday school attendance were mandatory. Catalog of Wilberforce University, 1874–74 (Xenia, Ohio: n. p., 1873), pp. 25–28.

[2]Mary Church Terrell, *A Colored Woman in a White World* (Washington, D.C.: Randell Publishing Co., 1940), pp. 61–62.

[3]David A. Gerber, "Ohio and the Color Line: Discrimination and Negro Responses in a Northern State, 1860–1915" (Ph.D. diss., Princeton University, 1971), pp. 21–26.

[4]Thomas Jesse Jones's 1916 monumental survey of black education, shows no parallel situation in either the South or the North.

[5]*Cleveland Gazette*, December 1, 1888; Frederick A. McGinnis, "A History of Wilberforce University." Ph.D. Dissertation, University of Cincinnati, 1940, pp. 105–110, 128; "Wilberforce University, the Combined Normal and Industrial Department, Their Relationship, Organic Ills, and their Remedy," typescript, William Sanders Scarborough Papers, Carnegie Library, Wilberforce University, is an excellent statement from the university's point of view of its claims to organic unity with the combined normal and industrial department.

[6]*Cleveland Gazette*, March 26, 1887.

[7]*Cleveland Gazette*, May 2, 1885.

[8]*Cleveland Gazette*, March 7, 1891; *New York Age*, March 21, 1891.

[9]*Cleveland Gazette*, April 25, 1891; *Columbus Ohio State Journal*, April 26, 29, 1891.

[10]*Cleveland Gazette*, March 7, April 18, 1891.

[11]A list of the men and women serving on the board of trustees from 1939 to the year of this publication appears in Appendix B.

Chapter 2

[1]*The Gold Torch*, September 28, 1978. Quote from a speech by Wesley delivered September 26, 1978.

[2]Amended Ohio Senate Bill No. 58, an act effective on and after August 19, 1941.

[3]Wesley to Ransom, May 19, 1942, Carnegie Library, Wilberforce University, Xenia, Ohio.

[4]Bishop R.R. Wright, Jr., Report to the Joint Executive Committee [June 6, 1942], Chicago, Ill., p. 5.

[5]Wright, Report, p. 6.

[6]Wright, Report, p. 8.

[7]Charles Wesley, "Conditions of Acceptance," 1942.

[8]"Minutes of the Executive Committee of the Board of Trustees," Howard University, June 10, 1942, pp. 2–3. The committee appointed Dr. Rayford Logan, professor of history, to the acting positions of dean of the Graduate School and head of the Department of History for the period of one year. Dr. Merze Tate was then temporarily appointed as associate professor of history for one year while Wesley was on leave. She was reappointed as was Dr. Logan. Minutes, (Executive Committee of the Boards of Trustees, Howard University, October 25, 1943, p. 1.)

[9]Wesley to Johnson, June 13, 1942.

Notes to Chapter 2

[10]"Wilberforce Celebrates 87th Founders Day," *The Christian Recorder,* March 11, 1943, p. to come; "Personalities," *The Christian Recorder,* April 8, 1943, p. 5.

[11]"Wilberforce University Unconditionally Accredited," *The Christian Recorder* 95 (April 1943): 1; Wilberforce University Report of President Wesley to the University Board of Trustees, April 7, 1943, Carnegie Library, Wilberforce University.

[12]"715 Enrolled This Year at Wilberforce," *The Pittsburgh Courier,* October 16, 1943; "An African Museum at Wilberforce University," *The Christian Recorder* 95 June 3, 1943,: 1. Additional changes were instituted in the Wilberforce University High School which, through the establishment of a teacher-training unit, became a laboratory school for the College of Education. The school was expanded to include grades seven and eight. Vocational training was introduced as a one course requirement for all high school students. For this, the federal government granted the use of a building and equipment totalling $250,000. ("715 Enrolled," *Pittsburgh Courier,* October 16, 1943; "Outstanding Accomplishment,".) For a discussion of the reorganization, see *The Truth About Wilberforce,* p. 13.

[13]The idea of an African museum was introduced at Howard by Kelly Miller in 1938 and supported by Wesley. (Kelly Miller Papers, Manuscript Division, The Moorland Spingarn Research Center, Howard University, Box 1, Washington, D.C. According to Harold Lewis, acting chairman, Department of History, Howard University, Ralph Bunche also introduced the idea of an African Museum while teaching at Howard.

[14]Charles Wesley, "To Connectionalize Wilberforce," *The Christian Recorder* 95 (May 1943): 1–9.

[15]"Tubman Chides AME Church," *The Afro-American,* June 19, 1943.

[16]"Fight Made on Force Prexy," *The Afro-American,* August 5, 1944; "Wilberforce Dilemma." August 5, 1944.

[17]"Another Fight at Wilberforce," *Cleveland Call and Post,* May 19, 1945.

[18]"Ransom-Wesley Feud at Wilberforce Seethes," *Chicago Defender,* May 19, 1945.

[19]*Chicago Defender,* May 19, 1945.

[20]"Chips Down in Furor Over Wilberforce Bill," *Ohio State News,* June 9, 1945; "The Inside Story," June 9, 1945.

[21]Charles Wesley, "President Wesley Issues Statement Concerning Wilberforce," *The Christian Recorder,* 97 (May 24, 1945): 5.

[22]Charles S. Spivey, "What is the Issue at Wilberforce," *The Christian Recorder* 97 (June 14, 1945): 9.

[23]Board of Trustees College of Education and Industrial Arts, and the National Alumni Association, *The Truth About Wilberforce,* June 26, 1947.

[24]Wesley to Spingarn, October 9, 1944, (Arthur Spingarn Papers, Manuscript Division, Moorland-Spingarn Research Center, Box 6, Washington, D.C.)

[25]Wesley to Ernest Alexander, November 15, 1946.

[26]Davis, "Church and State."

[27]Davis, "Church and State." "Ransom, Wesley Feud," *Pittsburgh Courier,* May 17, 1947 (Hallie Q. Brown Library, Central State University, Wilberforce, Ohio).

[28]"Wesley President-Elect of Morgan for 9 Months," *The Afro-American,* May 8, 1948.

[29]"Wesley Cleared of AME Charges: Dispute on Name Settled," *Xenia Evening Gazette,* September 9, 1947.

[30]"Wesley Cleared," *Xenia Gazette.*

[31]"Dr. Charles Wesley Making Bid for Political Power in Force Fight," *Ohio State News*, July 5, 1947.

[32]"Daniels Bill Would Make 'Bad Situation Intolerable,' Claim," *Xenia Gazette*, January 29, 1951.

[33]"Lausche Vetoes Bill to Create Central State," *Xenia Gazette*, May 4, 1951.

[34]"On Wilberforce: Students Criticize Lausche," *Xenia Gazette*, May 5, 1951; "Central State College and Wilberforce University Now Exist as Separate Schools," May 9, 1951.

[35]Du Bois to Wesley, June 10, 1932,

Chapter 3

[1]The Ohio State Board of Regents, *Basis of Data Series: Ohio Higher Education System* (Columbus: Board of Regents, 1981), pp. 12, 17. Other statistics in this and succeeding chapters may be found in the *Basis of Data Series*.

[2]Dean Howard H. Long to James T. Henry, Chairman, Committee on Future Planning, May 17, 1954.

[3]Harry G. Johns, interview with author, October 27, 1982. Other of Mr. Johns's remembrances of college life appear throughout the book.

[4]Pickett to Wesley, June 4, 1963.

[5]Wesley to Pickett, n.d. 1963.

[6]Leonora C. Lane, interview by Joseph D. Lewis May 26, 1976.

[7]Arthur D. Pickett, address to the Central State College faculty, May 23, 1963.

[8]U.S. Department of Commerce, Office of the Assistant Director for Statistical Standards, *Statistical Abstract of the United States*, 1952, p. 137; *Digest of Educational Statistics*, 1966; "Federal Programs of Education," p. 95.

[9]*The Gold Torch*, April 1965.

[10]For a representative year, 1955–56, resident student fees stood at $199 for three quarters and student workers' salaries at $150. Wesley, "Report of the President," 1950, p. 65; Ohio Board of Regents, *Basis of Data Series*, p. 27.

[11]Wesley, "Report of the President," 1956, p. 89. Emphasis added.

[12]Wesley, "Creating a Campus Climate," p. 10; Long to Henry May 17, 1954.

[13]Wesley, "Report of the President," 1956, p. 17; "Creating a Campus Climate," pp. 1, 21.

[14]Wesley, "Report of the President," 1956, p. 16.

[15]Wesley, "Creating a Campus Climate," p. 4.

[16]*The Gold Torch*, October 1965.

[17]*The Gold Torch*, October 1962.

[18]*The Gold Torch*, June 1961.

[19]Wesley, "Creating a Campus Climate," p. 3. Subsequent pages contain quotes from the 1960–61 conduct code and Wesley's published comments on the code.

[20]*The Gold Torch*, November 1965.

[21]*The Gold Torch*, September 1965.

[22]Wesley, "Creating a Campus Climate," p. 4.

[23]*The Gold Torch*, March 1965.

Notes to Chapter 4

[24]Quentin Burgess, "Tribute to Dr. Wesley," *The Negro History Bulletin*, 1965, p. 102.
[25]Wesley, "Creating A Campus Climate," p. 8.
[26]Wilbur Allen Page, "A Tribute to Dr. Charles H. Wesley, President, Central State College," *The Negro History Bulletin*, 28, (February 1965): 104.
[27]*The Gold Torch*, October 1963.
[28]*The Gold Torch*, April 1957.
[29]*The Gold Torch*, October 1963; January 1961.
[30]Wesley, "Creating a Campus Climate," p. 2; p. 8; p. 12.
[31]*The Gold Torch*, May 1961.

Chapter 4

[1]Lewis A. Jackson, interview with author, July 23, 1985. Subsequent quotes by Jackson are also from this interview.
[2]Harry E. Groves, interview with author, August 9, 1985. Subsequent quotes by Groves not otherwise identified are also from this interview.
[3]Harry E. Groves "Talk with the Faculty," December 7, 1965.
[4]Harry E. Groves, letter of resignation to the Board of Trustees of Central State University, November 25, 1967.
[5]Groves, "Talk with the Faculty."
[6]*Alumni Journal*, August 1966, p. 2.
[7]Alumni Journal, August 1966, p. 6.
[8]Harry E. Groves, "Talk with the Non-Academic Staff," December 7, 1965.
[9]Groves, "Talk with the Non-Academic Staff."
[10]Harry E. Groves, "The Present and Future Role of Predominantly Negro Institutions of Higher Education," convocation address, November 1, 1966, Central State University, Wilberforce, Ohio.
[11]Ibid. Groves, convocation, November 1, 1966.
[12]Harry E. Groves, "Inaugural Address," Central State University, Wilberforce, Ohio, October 21, 1966.
[13]Groves, convocation address, November 1, 1966.
[14]Harry E. Groves, "Talk with Students," December 7, 1965.
[15]Groves, "Talk with Students," December 7, 1965.
[16]Groves, convocation address, November 1, 1966.
[17]Harry E. Groves, "Convocation Speech," March 4, 1967, Central State University, Wilberforce, Ohio.
[18]Groves, letter of resignation, November 25, 1967.
[19]Groves's letter of resignation implies this, and this sentiment is echoed by faculty members who recall both selection processes. Groves states: "I have had the constant support of the board of trustees, of the chancellor of the board of regents and of the office of the governor." And he mentions by name several members of the legislature and the governor's cabinet. Henry Lee says of Branson, "I suppose the then Dean E. Oscar Woolfolk, a real close confidant of Branson may have had tremendous influence with the selection committee and the board. When Branson was away, Woolfolk was the strong hand on campus." (Interview with author, July 30, 1986.)

[20]*Alumni Journal,* Fall 1969, p. 1.

[21]Herman R. Branson, interview with author, August 5, 1985. Subsequent quotes by Groves are also from this interview.

[22]*Alumni Journal,* Fall 1967, p. 4.

[23]*Alumni Journal,* Winter 1970, p. 1.

[24]*Alumni Journal,* Spring 1970, p. 4.

[25]*Alumni Journal,* Fall 1969, pp. 4, 2.

[26]*Alumni Journal,* Winter 1970, p. 1.

[27]*Alumni Journal,* Fall 1969, pp. 5–8.

[28]*Alumni Journal,* Spring 1970, pp. 1, 17.

[29]Lewis A. Jackson, interview with author, July 23, 1985. Subsequent quotes by Jackson are also from this interview.

[30]*Alumni Journal,* Fall 1970, p. 1.

[31]It should be remembered that Central State had done a great deal during the Wesley administration to recruit and serve foreign students, and in 1971, faculty originated from Germany, Palestine, Iraq, the Phillippines, Yugoslavia, India, and several African nations.

[32]*Alumni Journal,* January 1972, pp. 1, 7.

Chapter 5

[1]Questionnaire completed by Jackson, July 1984.

[2]Questionnaire completed by Newsom, July 1984.

[3]*Alumni Journal,* June 1973, pp. 1–2.

[4]Michael J. Price, "Lionel Hodge Newsom: A Personal Perspective," *Sphinx,* Spring 1980, pp. 6–8. During Newsom's presidency of the fraternity, the headquarters was renovated, additional land purchased, and the organizational structure amended.

[5]Mary Snead Boger, *Charlotte 23* (Bassett, Va.: Bassett Printing Corp., 1972), p. 215.

[6]William Rouselle, "The Struggle to Save a Black School," *The Black Collegian,* April/May 1983, p. 44.

[7]Edward A. Jones, *A Candle in the Dark: A History of Morehouse College,* (Valley Forge, Penn.: Judson Press, 1967).

[8]Boger, p. 220.

[9]Polk Lafoon, student.

[10]*The Gold Torch,* May 2, 1974.

[11]*Alumni Journal,* June 1974, p. 1.

[12]William Rouselle, "The Struggle to Save a Black School", *The Black Collegean,* April/May 1983.

[13]*The Gold Torch,* May 2, 1974.

[14]*The Gold Torch,* May 2, 1974.

[15]*The Gold Torch,* May 2, 1974.

[16]Newsom questionnaire.

[17]*The Gold Torch,* May 2, 1974.

[18]*Alumni Journal,* Sept. 1975.

[19]*Alumni Journal,* March 1977, p. 3

[20]*Alumni Journal,* Sept. 1977, p. 6

Notes to Chapter 5

[21]The list of luminaries engaged for these weekly convocations is indeed impressive. It has included Hank Aaron, baseball great; Maya Angelou, writer, poet, and actress in the famous mini-series "Roots"; Lerone Bennett, senior editor of *Ebony* magazine; Ed Bradley, CBS television news White House correspondent and anchor of "CBS Sunday Night News"; Gwendolyn Brooks, Pulitzer Prize winning poet; Tony Brown, journalist, president of Tony Brown Productions, Inc., producer and host of public TV's syndicated series "Tony Brown's Journal"; Stokley Carmichael, organizer for the All-African People's Revolutionary Party; Rev. Benjamin F. Cavis, director of the United Church of Christ Commission on Racial Justice; John Henrik Clarke, poet, author, editor, and educator; Representative John Conyers, Jr., from Michigan's 1st Congressional Dist.; Dr. H. Douglas Covington, chancellor of Winston-Salem (North Carolina) State University; Ossie Davis, actor, director, and playwright and his wife, Ruby Dee, actress; Senator Sam J. Erwin of North Carolina; Marcia Ann Gillespie, editor-in-chief of *Essence* magazine; Nikki Giovanni, poet, social activist, columnist; Dr. Robert L. Green, dean of the College of Urban Development, Michigan State University; Dick Gregory, comedian and social activist; Dr. Frank W. Hale Jr., vice provost for Minority Affairs and professor of communications at The Ohio State University; Richard Hatcher, mayor of Gary, Indiana; A. Leon Higginbotham, Circuit Judge of U.S. Court of Appeals for the Third Circuit, Philadelphia; Jesse Jackson, national director, Operation P.U.S.H.; Robert E. Johnson, associate publisher and executive editor, *Jet* magazine; Johnny L. Jones, superintendent of schools for Dade County, Florida; Representative Parren J. Mitchell from Maryland's 7th Congressional District; Rosa Parks, mother of the Civil Rights movement whose actions prompted a year-long bus boycott in Montgomery, Alabama; Oliver Ocasek, Ohio State Senator and educational leader; Dr. Barbara Sizemore, associate professor of black studies at the University of Pittsburgh; Dr. Kenneth Tollett, director, Institute for the Study of Educational Policy at Howard University, Charles Wesley, former CSU president; Coleman A. Young, mayor of Detroit, Michigan.

[22]*Alumni Journal,* Sept. 1979.

[23]*The Gold Torch,* November 2, 1978.

[24]*The Gold Torch,* January 25, 1976.

[25]"The New Central State University," Central State University, Wilberforce, Ohio, 1978-79.

[26]Details regarding the museum are found in *The Gold Torch,* September 18, 1978; November 30, 1978; January 25, 1979; October 4, 1979; April 16, 1981; and December 2, 1982; *Alumni Journal,* March 1978, pp. 3-16; and September 1984, p. 2; and William Bower, "Jim Rhodes Leaves Mark With Blacks," *Toledo Blade.*

[27]*CSU News,* Spring Quarter, 1979/80, pp. 1-2.

[28]*The Gold Torch,* October 16, 1980; January 14, 1982 and April 22, 1982.

[29]*The Gold Torch,* April 16, 1981.

[30]*The Gold Torch,* April 23, 1984.

[31]*The Gold Torch,* January 22, 1981.

[32]*The Gold Torch,* January 22, 1981.

[33]*The Gold Torch,* January 21, 1982.

[34]*The Gold Torch,* January 21, 1982.

[35]*The Gold Torch,* May 20, 1982.

[36]*The Gold torch,* May 28, 1981.

[37]Reprinted in *Alumni Journal,* March, 1982, p. 5.

[38]*Alumni Journal*, June, 1981, p. 1.
[39]*The Gold Torch*, April 9, 1984.
[40]*The Gold Torch*, March 12, 1984.

Chapter 6

[1]North Central Association of Colleges and Secondary Schools, *Guide for the Evaluation of Institutions of Higher Learning* (Chicago: Commission of Colleges and Universities, 1965), p. 1. All further references to the association's guidelines may be found in this source.

[2]Harry G. Johns, interview with author, October 27, 1982. Subsequent quotes by Johns are also from this interview.

[3]Pickett to Wesley, May 5, 1964.

[4]*The Gold Torch*, March 1964.

[5]*The Gold Torch*, April 19, 1979.

[6]*The Gold Torch*, March 3, 1977.

[7]*The Gold Torch*, April 12, 1979.

[8]*CSU News*, Spring Quarter 1979/80.

[9]This excerpt and others have been provided by Dr. Joseph D. Lewis, then Director of Special Student Programs and Professor of History, Central State University. They are part of the as yet unpublished "Oral History: The Negro in the Making of America," which Dr. Lewis is compiling from interviews with guest lecturers in his course of the same name. They are unpaginated. (Mildred Henderson, interview with author, May 11, 1976.)

[10]James T. Henry, interview with author, July 30, 1986.

[11]Walter G. Sellers, interview with author.

[12]Johns, interview.

[13]*Alumni Journal*, April 1966, p. 13.

[14]North Central, *Guide*, p. 19.

[15]Lewis A. Jackson, interview with author, Xenia, Ohio, November 3, 1982. Subsequent quotes by Jackson are also from this interview.

[16]*Alumni Journal*, Fall 1969, p. 7.

[17]Paul McStallworth, interview with author, Wilberforce, Ohio, November 8, 1982. Subsequent quotes by McStallworth are also from this interview.

[18]Professor James T. Henry, Sr., interview with author, July 30, 1986.

[19]Herman Branson, interview with author, July 17, 1986.

[20]James T. Henry, Sr., interview with author, Xenia, Ohio, October 23, 1982. Subsequent quotes by Henry are also from this interview.

[21]*Alumni Journal*, Fall 1969, p. 6.

[22]*Alumni Journal*, Spring 1979, p. 4.

[23]James T. Henry, interview with author, July 30, 1986.

[24]Wilhelmina Robinson, telephone interview with author, October 29, 1982.

[25]A retirement roster, reprinted in Appendix, compiled in 1973 further illustrates the loyalty and longevity of service of both faculty and staff members.

[26]A complete list of persons who have received honorary degrees may be found in Appendix.

[27]Leonora C. Lane, interview by Joseph D. Lewis, May 26, 1976.

[28]*Alumni Journal,* June 1977, p. 10.

[29]*Alumni Profiles* were compiled in 1977, and an updated version is scheduled for release sometime in 1987. Appendix lists the persons who have been honored as alumnus of the year 1970–1986. Appendix lists the men and women who have served as General Alumni Association presidents.

[30]On February 28, 1980, Seller's service to both Central and the surrounding community were recognized through the awarding of the F.M. Torrence Award for Community Service. (See *Alumni Journal,* June 1980.)

[31]Walter G. Sellers, interview with author, Wilberforce, Ohio, October 15, 1982. It is also interesting to note that Sellers, his wife, and three children have graduated from Central State.

Chapter 7

[1]Arthur E. Thomas, interview with author, July 1985.

[2]*Alumni Journal,* December 1985, p. 5 and March 1986, p. 4.

[3]*The Gold Torch,* March 13, 1986.

[4]*Alumni Journal,* March 1986, p. 5.

[5]*The Gold Torch,* June 15, 1986.

[6]*The Gold Torch,* June 15, 1986.

[7]Tim Goffney, "Plan May Give CSU Role in Building Space Station," *The Journal Herald,* Dayton, Ohio, May 14, 1986.

[8]Arthur E. Thomas, *Central State University Enhancement Programs for the 21st Century: A Six Year Plan,* May 1986.

[9]*The Gold Torch,* October 24, 1985.

[10]James Crawford, "Black Leaders' Group Backs Nontraditional Language Curriculum" *Education Week,* January 8, 1986, pp. 4–5, 16.

[11]Crawford, "Black Leaders."

[12]*The Gold Torch,* June 15, 1986.

[13]*The Gold Torch,* May 2, 1985.

[14]*The Gold Torch,* June 15, 1986.

[15]A full-color catalog, *Ohio African-American Artists Showcase 1986,* has been printed and may be obtained from the university.

[16]*The Gold Torch,* May 2, 1985.

[17]*Jet,* April 21, 1986, pp. 22–24; *Alumni Journal,* March 1986, p. 3; *Jet,* February 24, 1986, pp. 23–24.

Index

Index

Index

Index

University Mothers. *See* National Association of Central State University Mothers
University of Cincinnati, 77, 103
University of Illinois, Chicago, 36
University of Michigan, 91
University of Singapore, 69
University of the State of New York, 23
Upton, Gertrude, 160
Upward Bound Program, 72, 99, 100, 107
Urban Education Project (Cincinnati), 105
U.S. Department of Education, 114
U.S. Department of Transportation, 110

Vann, Arlene T., 98
Vath, Charles G., 153
Veterans Upward Bound Program, 107

Wade, James S., 151, 152
Walcutt, Roscoe, 149
Walker Gym, 100
Walker, Ormonde, 23
Walker, Sammye S., 159
Walker, William O., 107, 150
Wallace, W. T., 8, 9
Walls, Jean H., 157
Walls, Lucille, 161
Waring, James H. N., Jr., 149
Washington, Booker T., 8
Washington, Dwight, 153
Washington University, St. Louis, 91
Waterman, Robert H., Jr., 144
Webber, Warren, 84
Wesley, Charles H.: academic career, 20; African studies program, 55; appeal for church funds, 23; on banning segregation, 67; becomes president, Wilberforce University, 20; board of trustees report on college environment, 53; church vs., 28; conditions of (presidential) acceptance, 19; on cultural atmosphere, 54–55; early accomplishments, 22–23; effect on alumni development, 136; effect on growth and expansion, 32; effect on teachers' salaries, 125–26; on faculty and administrators as role models, 59; on faculty support, 128; farsightedness of, 65–67; feud with Ransom, 27; and Fisk presidency, 26–27; on the gifted and tal-

ented, 56; idealism of, 36; impact on familial university structure, 117–21; nominated for Wilberforce presidency, 17; paternalism of, 123, 129; photograph as president, 21; and Pickett, letters of, 36–37; planning, 66; on the presidency, 24–26; as president, 1947–51, 31; as president, College of Education and Industrial Arts, 28; publications and awards, 61–62; on racial issues, 53, 65; on religion in college, 57; as shaper of institution's character, 61; and state boards, 24; on student discipline, 59–60; student fees payment policy, 38
Wesley Foundation, 58
West, Arlesia, 159
Westminster Club, 58
West, Raymond, 159
West, Thomas, 161
Whalen, Charles, Jr., 150
White, Carl, 141
White, Herbert, 157
White, Paul, 161
White, Walter, 148
Wilberforce State College, 29
Wilberforce University: accreditation of, 22; AME funding of, 3, 9; begun, 1; as Central State College, effect of name change, 30, 32, 41; College of Education and Industrial Arts at, 18; Combined Normal and Industrial Department at, 5; as CSU sister school, 96–97; familial structure of, 117; Joint Executive Committee, 18; and Wilberforce State College, 29
Wilkins, Roy, 149
Williams, Ernestyne, 160
Williamson, Anne, 159
Willis, Haywood, 157
Willis, Herbert, 161
Willis, J. Walter, 149
Wingard, Edward L., 104–5
Wood, Jesse L., 153
Woodrow Wilson Foundation, 92
Woodson, Dr. Carter G., 61
Woodson, George F., Jr., 159
Woolfolk, E. Oscar, 81, 82, 123, 126, 159
Wray, Nerissa, 161

180